Cambridge Elements

Elements in Political Philosophy
edited by
Cécile Laborde
University of Oxford
Steven Wall
University of Arizona

POLITICS AND THE ECONOMY

Lisa Herzog
University of Groningen

Shaftesbury Road, Cambridge CB2 8EA, United Kingdom

One Liberty Plaza, 20th Floor, New York, NY 10006, USA

477 Williamstown Road, Port Melbourne, VIC 3207, Australia

314–321, 3rd Floor, Plot 3, Splendor Forum, Jasola District Centre, New Delhi – 110025, India

103 Penang Road, #05–06/07, Visioncrest Commercial, Singapore 238467

Cambridge University Press is part of Cambridge University Press & Assessment, a department of the University of Cambridge.

We share the University's mission to contribute to society through the pursuit of education, learning and research at the highest international levels of excellence.

www.cambridge.org
Information on this title: www.cambridge.org/9781009592468
DOI: 10.1017/9781009592451

© Lisa Herzog 2025

This publication is in copyright. Subject to statutory exception and to the provisions of relevant collective licensing agreements, no reproduction of any part may take place without the written permission of Cambridge University Press & Assessment.

When citing this work, please include a reference to the DOI 10.1017/9781009592451

First published 2025

A catalogue record for this publication is available from the British Library

ISBN 978-1-009-59246-8 Hardback
ISBN 978-1-009-59241-3 Paperback
ISSN 2976-5706 (online)
ISSN 2976-5692 (print)

Cambridge University Press & Assessment has no responsibility for the persistence or accuracy of URLs for external or third-party internet websites referred to in this publication and does not guarantee that any content on such websites is, or will remain, accurate or appropriate.

For EU product safety concerns, contact us at Calle de José Abascal, 56, 1°, 28003 Madrid, Spain, or email eugpsr@cambridge.org

Politics and the Economy

Elements in Political Philosophy

DOI: 10.1017/9781009592451
First published online: November 2025

Lisa Herzog
University of Groningen

Author for correspondence: Lisa Herzog, l.m.herzog@rug.nl

Abstract: In today's societies, political and economic issues are closely intertwined, and political philosophy has turned more and more to economic issues. This Element introduces some key questions of economic philosophy: How to think about the relation between political and economic power? Can markets be 'tamed'? Which values are embedded in the economy and how do those relate to political values? It answers these questions by considering arguments from three theoretical perspectives – liberal egalitarian approaches, neo-republicanism, and critical theory or socialist thought – explaining their different background assumptions but also shared grounds. To illustrate these topics, it zooms in on the future of work: How could work be made more just, democratic, and sustainable? In the conclusion, some implications for research strategies in economic philosophy are explored.

Keywords: Economic philosophy, markets, property, democracy, philosophy of work

© Lisa Herzog 2025

ISBNs: 9781009592468 (HB), 9781009592413 (PB), 9781009592451 (OC)
ISSNs: 2976-5706 (online), 2976-5692 (print)

Contents

1 Introduction 1

2 Economic and Political Power 13

3 Work between Politics and Economics 35

4 Conclusion 56

References 61

1 Introduction

1.1 Political Philosophy and the Economy

In spring 2020, politicians in many countries took a drastic decision: they imposed lockdowns on their populations, to prevent the spread of the Covid-19 virus. This had huge effects on the economy: many businesses were threatened by bankruptcy; restaurants struggled to switch to take-out models; in India, thousands of migrant workers returned from the cities to their villages. This example shows that political decisions can have a massive impact on the economy. But economic events can also have a massive impact on politics. Take the 2008 Great Financial Crisis: it threw into disarray not only financial markets and major banks but also the lives of millions of citizens, in the United States and elsewhere, who could no longer afford their mortgages. In the subsequent economic downturn, many countries got into trouble repaying their debts and some governments fell for that reason. There was a lot of public discussion about the justifiability of the bailout of the banks, and about why, in most countries (except Iceland), top bankers were not held to account.

As these cases make clear, political and economic developments are closely intertwined. This is true not only in exceptional situations such as financial or public health crises but at any moment in time. Think about local politics, for example, the government of a city. One way in which politics is dependent on economic developments is resources: typically, some part of local governments' budget comes from local taxes, so how well local businesses are doing is important for politics. Measures taken by politicians, in turn, have an impact on economic actors. For example, turning a street into a pedestrian zone, to cut down car traffic and CO_2 emissions, will affect local businesses. This is why they will most likely make their voices heard when such decisions are taken. In fact, politicians might anticipate the reactions of economic actors to policy proposals. If these actors are powerful, the proposals might not even be put on the agenda. It seems clear that to understand local politics, one needs to understand both its political and its economic dimensions (and other dimensions as well, e.g., local culture, religion, etc.). The same holds if one wants to normatively evaluate such politics, for example, by discussing how just or unjust its outcomes are. And it holds not only on the local but also on the regional, national, and international level.

And yet, political philosophy has long neglected the economy.[1] It mostly focused on the philosophical underpinnings *of politics*, and often left aside

---

[1] This *Element* focuses on Western philosophy, which should of course not be assumed to be the only possible perspective. However, given that Western economic thinking and economic practices had a large, and often negative, impact on other world regions, it is all the more important to

questions about economic phenomena. If one looks at the table of contents of textbooks in political philosophy, economic issues will often appear only as sub-topics, or not at all. With this, political philosophy follows the broader division of academic labour, in which economics and politics are mostly treated as two separate fields of inquiry.[2] The assumption behind this separation is that each field can focus on one particular social sphere, holding constant what happens in other spheres. According to this picture, economics explores phenomena such as markets, business cycles, or monetary systems, without discussing politics explicitly, only assuming that governments would secure property rights and enforce contracts. Political science, in turn, explores issues such as election cycles, or the relation between media and party politics, without considering economic developments. Of course, this picture is simplified, and various line of research, for example, on welfare economics and welfare politics, have explored the intersection of economic and political dimensions with regard to specific topics. But as a matter of academic sociology (e.g. when looking at job descriptions, conference topics, or the scope of academic journals), a considerable amount of research continues to treat political and economic issues separately.

Political philosophy has often followed this model, understanding its task as reflecting on the political dimensions of society, and on the principles that should govern them. Of course, these have indirect implications for the economy. For example, if one explores the nature of the public sphere and of democratic discourse, one needs to assume that *there can be* such a sphere of free political discussion, and that it is not, for example, completely dominated by commercial speech. And yet, economic dimensions were often not at the centre of attention.

What may also have contributed to the marginalization of economic issues in political philosophy is the perception that economics concerns instrumental means-ends relations, whereas political philosophy concerns values and principles, and is thus logically prior: one first needs to know what kind of society one wants, governed by which values and principles, and then one can leave it to the economists to think about the institutional implementation. This approach, however, suffers from a basic problem: without knowing what economic institutions are feasible, and what effects they have on the wider society, one does not know what kind of society might be possible. One might err in two ways: one might be too utopian, thinking that certain values can be realized in harmony with each

---

critically engage with them. Engaging in a dialogue with non-Western thinking on economic issues, and learning from them, is an ongoing endeavour within economic philosophy and will hopefully grow in the future.

[2] Some exceptions are discussed in section 1.2 below.

other, but the empirical reality forces one to accept compromises between them. Or one might be too conservative, thinking that certain things need to be accepted as they currently are, while this is in fact not true and other institutional solutions are well possible. An integrated analysis, which considers political values and principles and the economic institutions for realizing them *together*, can better try to find a middle path between these two forms of error.

The model of a separate analysis of the political and economic sphere may have had some plausibility in an era such as the post-World War II era in the Western world, in which both the political and the economic system were largely national affairs. In such a situation, one may assume that politics 'sets the frame' for economic activities and gives the economic system the shape it wants it to have. In the social-democratic tradition, this was described by the slogan of 'the primacy of politics' (Berman, 2006). A lot of political philosophy, especially in the liberal-egalitarian camp (see Section 1.2.1), implicitly or explicitly assumed this to be case (Claassen and Herzog, 2019). But in today's world, it is questionable whether this assumption holds. A key problem is that the economy has been globalized: value chains span the globe, capital can easily travel internationally, and jobs can be shifted to other countries. Politics, in contrast, still takes place mostly at the national level. This has shifted the balance of power to economic actors, especially transnational corporations: they are internationally mobile and can threaten to leave any specific country if they disagree with political decisions, weakening the power of political actors.

For these reasons, an integrated perspective on politics and the economy is needed. When it comes to empirical research, the term 'political economy' is sometimes used to describe such a perspective (e.g. Acemoglou and Robinson, 2012). In philosophy, there is not yet a clearly established terminology. Sometimes, 'philosophy, politics and economics' (PPE), the name of degree courses at various universities, is also used as a designation for an integrated research perspective. I suggest the term 'economic philosophy' (which is shorter than 'political-economic philosophy' or 'philosophy of political economy') to describe the integrated normative analysis of political and economic institutions and practices.[3] The focus of this *Element* lies mostly on the macro-level of the political-economic system as a whole. A similar perspective can also be applied to the meso-level of societal organizations, or the micro-level of individual behaviour, but for reasons of space, I will not discuss these.[4]

---

[3] This terminology also aligns with 'philosophie économique' (in French) or 'Wirtschaftsphilosophie' (in German), which describe the same field of research.

[4] Another field in normative philosophy, business ethics, looks at economic phenomena at the level of individual behaviour or organizational structures. For reasons of space, I cannot discuss it here, but I accept the argument of those (e.g. Heath et al., 2010) who argue that political philosophy and

Defined in this way, 'economic philosophy' differs from the 'philosophy of economics' understood as the philosophy of science applied to economics.[5] The latter addresses the methodologies used in economic research from a philosophical perspective. It asks, for example, what an economic model is, and how to distinguish good from bad abstractions when developing models (e.g. Spiegler, 2015; Hausman, 2021, section 3). Such discussions can be relevant for economic philosophy in so far as they can contain important messages about the validity and strength of models and theories that economic philosophers might want to draw on. But overall, economic philosophy, as I understand it, is less interested in economics *as a field of inquiry* but more in economic institutions and practices *as social phenomena*. As such, it can draw not only on insights from economics but also from other academic fields that explore economic phenomena, for example economic sociology, economic psychology, or organization studies. One challenge for economic philosophers, however, is to make sure that they have a sufficient understanding of the methodologies and approaches used by these different fields, so that they can properly weigh their – sometimes conflicting – insights. Often, the best way of ensuring this is to collaborate with scholars from these fields. This is the way in which economic philosophers have proceeded in rethinking, for example, central banking and monetary politics (e.g. Dietsch et al., 2018; Heldt and Herzog, 2022). In what follows, I present three philosophical traditions from which economic institutions and practices have been discussed in recent years, in the nascent field of economic philosophy.

1.2 Three Philosophical Perspectives on the Economy

The 'default' perspective from which economic phenomena are often discussed is that of mainstream economics: neoclassical economics. Within political philosophy, some authors understand themselves as standing in the tradition from which it originated, namely the classical liberalism of David Hume, Adam Smith, and others (e.g. Tomasi, 2012). The family of libertarian views, which exist in a right and a left version, shares certain key assumptions with it as well (see van der Vossen and Christmas 2023). Right libertarianism starts from self-ownership in one's body, while left libertarianism adds the common ownership of certain resources, for example, the earth, which can lead to different political implications (see e.g. Vallentyne et al., 2005).

---

business ethics should collaborate more closely; they might even be understood as parts of the same endeavour (see also Herzog, 2018).

[5] The term is sometimes used more broadly; Hausman (2021) also includes ethics and philosophy of action. Another area that is sometimes included is the history of economic and philosophical thought and their relation.

Rather than trying to delineate these views in detail from each other, let me briefly note what they have in common. Starting from methodological individualism, they make the rights and preferences of individuals, including their property rights, a core foundation (e.g. Nozick, 1974). This can go hand in hand with strong assumptions about individual freedom and responsibility. All these views – with some qualifications in left libertarianism – support free markets and see the role of the government primarily in creating the conditions for market exchanges, for example, the enforcement of property rights. They see markets as places in which individuals can make use of their economic freedoms, but also as allocation mechanisms in which the knowledge and preferences of all participants are conveyed through the price mechanism, which can lead to greater efficiency (e.g. Hayek, 1945; for a critical discussion see Herzog, 2023, chap. 7).

This latter point relates these approaches also to neoclassical economics. The latter, however, is welfarist in nature, in the sense that its normative criterion is the efficient satisfaction of individual preferences. Interestingly, in this respect it shares important tenets with utilitarianism, with its focus on maximizing overall welfare. Classical liberal and libertarian views reject utilitarianism because they would not want to see individual rights sacrificed to the common good. Moreover, while neoclassical economics tends to work with *static* models, for example, the general equilibrium model of markets, some strands, especially in libertarian thought, emphasize the *dynamic* features of markets, which allow for change and innovation.

In recent years, the discussion about politics and the economy has to some extent still taken place from that perspective, but also, increasingly, from three other perspectives. These do not start from an overly individualistic account of human nature in the way neoclassical economics and related theories do. They are thus better in line with research in psychology, sociology, and other fields that emphasizes the social embeddedness of human beings and the important role of formal and informal institutions in shaping human interactions, including markets. Moreover, these three perspectives arguably offer more critical potential concerning the status quo, which has, to a considerable extent, been shaped by free-market thinking (e.g. Conway and Oreskes, 2023). I now turn to these three approaches: liberal egalitarianism, neo-republicanism, and critical theory and socialist thought.

1.2.1 The Liberal-Egalitarian Tradition

The liberal-egalitarian tradition builds on the seminal work by John Rawls (1971, 1993) and the ensuing discussions about principles and currencies of justice. Rawls had famously asked what 'principles of justice' the members of a society would agree on if they were to choose them from behind a 'veil of ignorance', not knowing their position in society (Rawls 1971, esp. sections 4, 24; Rawls 2001, esp. section 25). This led to the formulation of a set of principles of justice, including equal political and civic rights, equality of opportunity, and – particularly relevant for the economic realm – the justification of inequality only if it benefits the 'least well-off members of society', the famous 'difference principle' (Rawls 1971, chap. 11–13). One might think that this would immediately invite a discussion of the economic institutions in which these principles could best be realized, but only few authors (e.g. Doppelt 1981; Krouse and McPherson 1986) turned directly to this question.

Instead, the discussion moved mostly to the justifiability of these abstract principles, and to the 'currencies' of justice: What should the principles of distributive justice be *about?* Rawls had suggested a multidimensional bundle of 'primary goods' (see esp. Rawls 1982). Dworkin (1981a, 1981b, 2000), in contrast, suggested that a just distribution should concern resources. Other commentators suggested welfare as currency, thereby drawing a line to the older traditions of utilitarianism and to welfare economics, both of which operate in terms of a subjective notion of 'utility' (e.g. Harsanyi, 1975).

A famous criticism of Rawls's principles came from Cohen (e.g. 1997), who suggested that the difference has more radical consequences than Rawls had realized. In Cohen's reading, this principle justifies unequal incomes by referring to the possibility of talented individuals to force society to pay higher wages for their work, by threatening to work less or to work in less productive jobs. This, Cohen argued, should not be part of the principles of justice, and contradicts the ethos of justice that should prevail in a just society.[6] Yet other commentators, for example, Frankfurt (1987), rejected the idea that distributive justice should look at the *overall* distribution of incomes, holding that it should focus instead on the fight against poverty, so that everyone has *enough* for a decent life (hence the term 'sufficientarianism', see e.g. Shields, 2020).

An intense discussion turned around the role of *responsibility* in relation to unequal outcomes (e.g. Dworkin, 1981a, 1981b, 2000). Many people share the intuition that individuals' choices matter for distributive justice: If someone works harder and therefore earns more money than others, wouldn't this be in line with justice? And conversely, could reckless behaviour or the squandering of money

---

[6] I return to this discussion below, in Section 3.1.

justify that some individuals are poorer than others? This 'luck egalitarian' strand of theorizing turned on the delineation of 'choice' from 'circumstances' (e.g. Cohen, 1989). Against these attempts, Anderson pointed out that the core of Rawls' theory was the aim of creating a 'society of equals' (1999, 311). Her 'relational egalitarian' perspective focuses on the social relations between individuals, leading to discussions about the economic institutions that a 'society of equals' should have. Clearly, individuals who see each other as moral equals will not let each other fall below a certain minimum standard of material well-being (e.g. no one should go hungry, people should get a second chance in life, etc.). Social relations – and hence also economic relations – should not be marked by domination or submission but should reflect the equal status of all members of society. This is compatible with a functional differentiation of roles and some material differences, but not with forms of inequality that undermine the equal standing of all citizens.[7] While some relational egalitarian approaches – including Anderson's (1999) famous article – focus mostly on the imperative to ensure a decent *minimum* for all members of society, others (e.g. Schemmel, 2021) are more demanding with the *overall degree* of inequality that they see as compatible with egalitarian principles.

The different liberal-egalitarian principles and currencies of justice can all be applied to questions about the economy. But it is worth noticing a distinction here between 'ideal' and 'non-ideal' theorizing (see Valentini, 2012 for an overview). While the terms get used in different ways, a helpful approach is to think about 'ideal theory' as asking what an ideally just society would do with regard to economic institutions and practices, and about 'non-ideal theory' as exploring possible improvements that start from the here and now, to make existing institutions and practices more just.

With regard to the economy as a whole, ideal theory has explored in quite some detail the two economic systems that Rawls had named as possible implementations of his theory of justice: liberal socialism and property-owning democracy (Rawls, 1971, 241–242; 1999, sections 41–43). The former describes an economic system with public ownership of the means of production (though not necessarily in the form of central planning at the national level) (Edmundson 2017; O'Neill 2020b; for related views see e.g. Schweickart, 2011; Adler, 2019). The latter assumes that economic decisions are taken mostly by

---

[7] When using the term "citizens," I use it as synonymous to "member of society," not in the more specific sense of "holder of a passport of the relevant country." There are many difficult questions about the position of individuals who are members of a society, but do not hold citizenship status. These questions are also relevant for economic philosophy, because such individuals often suffer from dire economic conditions (see e.g. Apostolidis, 2018 on migrant workers in the United States). For reasons of space, however, I here cannot discuss them here.

private individuals, in a decentralized system coordinated by markets, but that the dichotomy between capital owners and workers is overcome by a wide spreading of ownership of capital among all members of society (e.g. Thomas, 2017). Non-ideal theory turned, for example, to questions about racial discrimination in today's social and economic systems and what could be done to overcome it (e.g. Anderson, 2013).

In such discussions, liberal egalitarians tend to assume that politics can and should set the framework within which the economy operates. Their normative principles, or more applied normative recommendations, can be understood as addressing democratic citizens and to provide them with arguments about how to think about justice and how to implement just policies. Citizens can take up these arguments in their private reflections and in public discourse; once they have formed well-grounded opinions, they can vote for political parties that would implement reforms along these lines. For example, once a certain degree or type of inequality has been considered just, citizens can see whether the system of taxation and redistribution in their country comes close to it, and which party is most likely to move it into the right direction. Similarly, other regulations that have an impact on distributive outcomes,[8] for example, rules about minimum wages, can be evaluated against the principles of justice one has argued for, and citizens can come to considered judgements about which party to vote for on this basis.

This conceptual reliance on a well-functioning system of democratic governance might be seen as a weakness of this approach. It assumes that the state (a) has the right *orientation* (following the democratic will of the people and their views on justice), (b) has the *power* to implement just policies (also against strong interest groups) and (c) has the *competence* to do so (e.g. through a non-corrupt, effective public administration). These assumptions may not be fulfilled in real life, raising the question of whether this approach can ever lead to real-life change. In response, liberal egalitarians might say that they are not only interested in implementation, but in what just principles *are*. However, the more their theorizing concerns questions about concrete economic institutions, the more urgent the question of implementation becomes. Delegating questions about economic and political power, and about the relation between politics and the economy more generally, to specific discussions, for example, about campaign finance reform, can then create problematic omissions.

---

[8] Hacker (2011) introduced the term "predistribution" for capturing the idea that various economic regulations – from antitrust to labour market regulation – have an impact on the distribution even *before* redistributive taxation happens – hence the term 'predistribution'. For critical discussions, however, see Dietsch, 2010 or O'Neill, 2020a.

1.2.2 The Neo-Republican Approach

The second theoretical orientation that has been used to analyse economic institutions, neo-republicanism, centres on the idea of individuals as free and equal citizens, understanding freedom as non-domination. No citizen should stand under the arbitrary will of another, that is, be dominated. It is not enough to *in fact* have freedom to do what one wants, but one needs to have *guarantees* for it. The paradigmatic example used to illustrate this point is that of a liberal slaveholder who gives their slaves lots of freedom – and yet they remain slaves, without any guarantees of their rights and with no say in decisions about the rules they live by (e.g. Pettit, 1997). In this tradition, there is a strong focus on counter-power, checks and balances, and the active role that citizens need to play in upholding the institutions through which they govern themselves. It thereby links to different strands in the history of political thought (e.g. Cicero, Machiavelli, or Arendt) than the liberal tradition (where links are often drawn to Locke or Kant).

When applied to the economy and its relation to politics, this perspective leads to a distinct focus on power: Who holds power over whom, and how could such power be held in check? A key question that applies both to the political and to the economic realm is how to prevent domination, both in the interpersonal sense (person A dominating person B) and in the structural sense (social structures allowing person A to dominate person B, or the structures themselves dominating person B) (e.g. Gädeke, 2020). This perspective can, for example, be applied to the relation between employers and workers, as individuals or as groups. As such, it can also be related to distributive outcomes, with injustices such as exploitation being understood as resulting from domination (Vrousalis, 2023). Another interesting question is the way in which different *countries* might stand in relations of domination to each other, for example, because of one-sided dependencies in trade, or because the international monetary system relies on certain global currencies (Herzog, 2021).

A third topic that flows from the neo-republican perspective concerns power and counter-power in their relation to economic positions, especially wealth and poverty. This is relevant for thinking, for example, about the position of poor citizens and the eventual need for specific representation to safeguard their interests (e.g. Cagé, 2020), or about the role of strikes as a tool of working-class power (Gourevitch, 2018). Moreover, institutional proposals that liberal egalitarians might endorse for the sake of more just distributive outcomes can be considered from an explicit power perspective. For example, take a public job guarantee (e.g. Tcherneva, 2020), which liberal egalitarians might consider as an instrument of social insurance that provides incomes to unemployed individuals. From a neo-republican perspective, it is also an instrument of counter-power that provides employees with an exit option and thus makes it possible for them to stand up against their employers and to voice their concerns (Herzog, 2022).

Among neo-republican approaches that analyse economic institutions, one can distinguish different branches: liberal-republican ones, which see neo-republicanism as an advancement of liberal-egalitarian thought, or socialist or 'radical' republican ones that connect more closely to socialist thought. While the former (e.g. Thomas, 2017) take normative individualism as their starting point and have a more positive view of (well-regulated) markets, the latter tend to be more sceptical of markets and focus more on social classes or other collective units (e.g. Al Salman, 2022). This connects them to critical theory and socialist thought, the third philosophical tradition in which many contributions to economic philosophy have been made.

1.2.3 Critical Theory and Socialist Thought

The term 'critical theory', as originally defined by Horkheimer (1937/1968), designates a form of theorizing that does not aim at *describing* the social world as it exists at a certain point in time, but that works towards change, to overcome domination and oppression and to create a more just society. As such, it stands in line with Marx's famous eleventh thesis on Feuerbach that philosophers had tried to understand the world, but the point is to change it (Marx, 1845/1969). Of course, Marxist and socialist thought is itself an extremely rich and multifaceted tradition (Kołakowski, 2008). While some of its strands fall squarely into economic theory, others belong to political thinking and philosophy. Among the latter, one can distinguish between approaches that analyse economic institutions, and those that analyse broader political or cultural phenomena, often from the perspective of 'ideology critique', in the tradition of Gramsci, Althusser, and others (Gilabert and O'Neill, 2024).

A particular focus in this tradition lies on analysing the power relations that stem from economic relations and from the ownership of the means of production. The latter are often in the hands of a small group of people, while the majority of the population need to generate an income through work. Typically, there is an imbalance of power between these groups, because workers are more dependent on their income than capitalists are dependent on any specific worker, at least as long as there is an 'industrial reserve army' of unemployed individuals (Engels, 1845/1969). This imbalance is seen as the last stage in a longer historical trajectory in which there is always an opposition between social classes, for example, feudal lords and servants in medieval Europe. When capitalism developed, the decisive class division became that between bourgeois capital owners and proletarian workers. Writing in the mid-nineteenth century, Marx, Engels, and their followers expected that a revolution was imminent, because the internal contradictions of the capitalist system would lead to its implosion, with the proletarians taking power. But – to cut a very complex story short – in the advanced capitalist countries, this did not happen. A revolution that understood itself as 'socialist' took place, and a new economic system was implemented, in Russia, which was still largely agrarian at the time. In the capitalist countries in Western Europe and the United States, in contrast, socialist and social-democratic parties slowly gained some political power by organizing protests and strikes and winning seats in parliaments. From the perspective of radical Marxists, however, this meant an accommodation to the status quo without a fundamental shift of the economic power relations of capitalism.

Behind this judgement stands the assumption that political power relations ultimately always follow economic power relations. The former cannot be an independent counterpower to the latter because without property in the means of production, politicians cannot stand up against capitalists. Modern politics, in other words, is nothing but the 'superstructure' of the capitalist economy (Marx, 1859/1971). This can be understood as a form of domination: capitalists dominate the rest of society and do not even have to actively exercise this power. The mere possibility of, say, a corporation cutting jobs can be enough for politicians to take certain policy proposals off the agenda. Moreover, corporations and their owners can also have an influence on politics through the ownership of media, the framing of public discourse, and other indirect means – hence the interest of critical theorists in ideology and the cultural dimensions of capitalism.

A key point of discussion between critical theorists, liberal-egalitarians, and neo-republicans – apart from questions about diverging values and principles – is whether this picture of politics as nothing but a 'superstructure' to economic relations is an adequate description of reality. For example, to what extent can other forms of power provide a counterpower to that of capital owners? What changes if the role of unions, as collective organizations of workers, is taken into account (a phenomenon that did not yet exist on a large scale at the time when Marx and Engels were writing)? Is meaningful reform possible through democratic politics, or is the latter condemned to always remain at the surface? What hope for change, then, is there at all?

Critical theorists have often criticized other strands of political thinking for being insufficiently radical in their demands. For example, Marxist feminism – as developed out of Marx's original thought, which was not concerned with gender issues – has charged liberal feminism with being insufficiently attuned to the question of class among women (e.g. Fraser, 2013). Marxist or critical ecological thought argues that a true shift in our relation to nature requires overcoming the capitalist system, in which nature always remains a 'resource' to be exploited (e.g. Barca, 2020). These strands of theorizing have also been taken up by many thinkers from the Global South, who criticize the expansionary dynamic of capitalism and the unjust economic relations between richer and poorer countries (e.g. Svampa, 2019). From this perspective as well, the call is to interrupt the expansionary and exploitative logic of capitalism.

Which of these lines of thought has the strongest arguments in its favour when it comes to thinking about the relation between politics and the economy? Liberal egalitarianism has the advantage of starting from general, widely accepted premises, whereas the premises, both normative and with regard to the assumptions about society, of neo-republicanism and critical theory are somewhat more specific. On the other hand, the discussions of liberal egalitarianism may sometimes appear too abstract, at a distance from the empirical realities of economic power and the obvious injustice of many existing economic institutions and practices. Neo-republicanism adds an important dimension by focussing on the status of free citizens and the institutions that are needed to uphold this status for all members of society. Socialist thought, meanwhile, often pushes for thinking about true alternatives to the current status quo, even though this in turn raises difficult questions about their political feasibility (on questions of transition see, e.g., Gilabert and O'Neill, 2024, section 5).

When it comes to many current economic practices and institutions, however, thinkers from the different traditions can come to similar conclusions, despite the deeper differences in their orientations. Many wrongs that take place in today's economic system are normatively overdetermined. Take, for example, the huge material inequalities that exist in many countries. These are distributively unjust according to almost all theories of distributive justice from the liberal-egalitarian camp. They create situations of domination and unfreedom, as neo-republicans criticize them. And they reinforce the tendency of political power to follow economic power, a point that socialists focus on.

Similarly, certain proposals of reform can be endorsed from different normative standpoints. For example, a universal basic income or a public job guarantee can be seen as reducing poverty and hence as an improvement in distributive justice, as reducing the domination of workers by capitalists and hence increasing neo-republican freedom, or as interrupting the capitalist dynamics of wages and working conditions being always pushed down as much as possible. Thus, even though many differences remain – in the underlying world views, in the accounts of human nature, and in assumptions about the social relations in the economic and political realm – for many points of critique, agreements (or at least pragmatic coalitions) between these three camps are possible.

1.3 Preview

In the following sections, an integrated perspective on politics and the economy will be presented, focusing on a number of topics. Of course, given the length of this *Element*, readers cannot expect a comprehensive account of 'the economy'. Instead, what informed the choice of topics was to ask which issues provide good illustrations for the value of such an integrated approach. The next section discusses economic and political power and their interplay, with three thematic focuses: the question whether markets can be 'tamed', the role of property rights in the economic system, and the role of democratic values in the economy.

The third section focuses on a more applied topic, namely the future of work, which it addresses on both ideal and non-ideal levels of theorizing. This issue is currently also hotly debated in public discourse, not least because of technological developments, for example, in artificial intelligence, which challenge the nature of many jobs. It is, moreover, a topic that does not require a long technical introduction of the kind that would be needed for, say, a discussion of the global monetary system. Work affects all of us, even those who do not work for pay, which means that most people have a good sense of what contemporary working conditions are like. How work is organized is thus a key question at which political and economic arguments intersect. The section presents the discussions about wage justice and workplace democracy and asks how the future of work relates to a future that is also environmentally sustainable. The conclusion summarizes some central points and identifies key research areas for inter- and transdisciplinary approaches in economic philosophy.

2 Economic and Political Power

A key question when thinking about the relation between politics and the economy is that of power. Political institutions create positions of power: for example, members of parliament can, if they organize a majority, enact laws that have far-ranging impacts on other members of society. In the economy, one also finds positions that one intuitively associates with power: for example, a CEO can decide about thousands of jobs being created or destroyed, or a union leader can initiate a ballot to call a strike. But how do these forms of power relate to each other? Taking up elements from the three approaches – liberal-egalitarian, neo-republican and socialist thought – described in Section 1, this section presents an integrated perspective on economic and political power.

Questions of power have often been discussed separately in the mainstream of political philosophy, rather than being integrated into all discussions. The liberal-egalitarian camp has in fact been criticized by so-called 'realist' theorists that it neglects questions of power (for an overview see Rossi and Sleat, 2014). Many economic theories are also silent on power; in the words of Lukes, economists 'have little, and usually nothing, to say about the concept of power, about what power is, and how to study it' (Lukes, 2016: 17). This might have to do with the fact that a lot of economic theory is organized around the ideal of a fully competitive market (in contrast to, say, a monopoly), in which all participants are assumed to choose according to their own preferences and prices are determined by the system as a whole; therefore, nobody can force others to behave in certain ways.

What, then, is power? The notion is itself notoriously contested, with a whole literature discussing the strengths and weaknesses of different conceptualizations (for an overview see, e.g., Dowding, 2011). Many accounts build, in one way or another, on the work of Max Weber, who had famously defined social power as 'the probability that one actor within a social relationship will be in a position to carry out his own will despite resistance' (Weber, 1968 [1921], I: 53). In a recent article, Rutger Claassen and I suggested the following working definition: power means 'being in a position to impose one's will on others' (Claassen and Herzog, 2021: 225, see also Allen, 1999). Power thus describes an opportunity or capacity; one can have power without exercising it.

In a famous categorization offered by Lukes, this is the 'first face' of power, based on decision-making (Lukes, 1974/2005). But it is not its only form, which is why Lukes also described two other 'faces'. The second is agenda setting: if other people anticipate that one might exercise one's power, they might, for example, not even put certain things on the agenda or dare to speak out about them (ibid., see also Bachrach and Baratz, 1962). Others might even adapt their behaviour to the will of those who have power *without the latter doing anything*, a phenomenon described as 'passive power' (Morris 2007, chap. 13). Thirdly, power can also influence individuals' beliefs and preferences, as when women in a patriarchal society do not develop preferences for certain jobs, as these seem out of reach for them (Lukes, 1974/2005). To understand power, one therefore cannot focus only on actual behaviours and outcomes but must also consider counterfactuals (what outcome *would* have been different, what other preferences *might* people have developed, etc., *if a specific form of power had not been there*).

Power typically has to do with the social positions that individuals hold, and with the resources, material and immaterial, that they possess. These social positions and resources, in turn, are part of broader social structures. If one looks at a situation in which one individual, for example, a boss, can exercise power over another, for example, an employee, one needs to take these broader structures into account. In this example, these can include labour law, unemployment rates, welfare state institutions, or the cultural meaning ascribed to paid work in a society. This is also why discussions about power (both descriptively, on where it lies, and normatively, on where it should lie or how it should be exercised) also need to take these different dimensions of social structures into account. Or to put it positively: a perspective of power allows one to *integrate* such different considerations. Moreover, it is often helpful to also take the *temporal* dimension into account: power constellations can shift over time, often in self-reinforcing processes (Claassen and Herzog, 2021). If a group of individuals has power over others, this allows them to change the social situation in ways that are beneficial to them, for example, by acquiring more resources or by enlarging the rights connected to their social positions. This can help them acquire more power, which in turn allows for more changes in the social structures, and so on.

This is one of the reasons why political philosophy has long thought about the ways in which there can be checks and balances between different positions of power, for example, between different political institutions. Montesquieu (1748/1989) had famously distinguished between the legislative, judicative, and executive branches of government. Questions about the power relations between different political institutions, for example, between parliaments as elected representatives of the citizenry and constitutional courts as defenders of the constitution, remain important topics for political philosophy (e.g. Lever, 2009). What gets addressed less, however, is the question of how these *political* power relations relate to *economic* power relations. What if a legislative institution, say the government of a state, wants to use its power to change the rules of doing business, for example by imposing stricter environmental regulations on certain industries? Are they in a position to 'impose their will on others', or would they not dare to do so, out of fear of companies reducing campaign donations, lobbying against them, or moving jobs to a different constituency?

In what follows, I will discuss this question by turning to three sub-questions. The first, which stays close to this example, concerns the question of whether markets can be 'tamed' by democratic politics and what this would mean. Then I zoom in on a specific topic that the traditions of critical theory and socialist thought have emphasized in particular: the role of property rights, and specifically of ownership in the means of production. As these two sections will show, the balance between political and economic power is often precarious, and it is not clear whether democratic politics is indeed in a position to 'impose its will' on economic actors. I conclude the section by suggesting that to change this situation for the better, democratic principles need to be embedded not only in the political rules that 'set the framework' for the economy but also within economic institutions themselves.

2.1 Can Markets Be 'Tamed'?

Markets, as institutions in which individuals exchange goods and services for money, have existed for centuries, including within societies the main economic logic of which was very different, for example, a feudal command economy. It was only during the nineteenth and twentieth century that they became the dominant logic of the economic realm. Also now, they are not the only economic logic, even though the term 'market economy' may suggest this. There are many activities that take place within the hierarchical logic of work organizations, with teams working together under the command of a boss. Other goods and services are produced by individuals for themselves or for their families. And there are public goods provided by governments at the local, regional, or national level, and provided to citizens on an egalitarian basis. The combination of these elements differs from society to society, putting them on different places on the spectrum from 'market economies' (in which the market is restricted to the economic sphere in a narrow sense) to 'market societies' (in which markets dominate all economic and social relations) (Polanyi, 1944; Cunningham, 2005).

What, then, are markets? They are mechanisms in which goods and services are allocated to those who are willing to pay for them, through formally voluntary exchanges. The price mechanism coordinates the supply and demand of goods: the price goes down if supply is greater than demand, and up if demand is greater than supply. This sends a signal to suppliers that they should adapt their supply, creating incentives for them to provide the goods or services that best serve the interests of buyers. At least this holds if there is perfect competition in markets, without the kind of one-sided market power, on either side, that can arise if the number of market participants is small. In a perfectly competitive market equilibrium, the price equals the marginal costs of production, meaning that consumers pay no more than is socially necessary for producing these goods or services. The result is 'Pareto-efficient' in the sense that no participant can improve their welfare without that of another participant being diminished – there is 'no waste' in the system (e.g. Mas-Colell et al., 1995: 313).

This, at least, is the theoretical model of markets that economists from Adam Smith onward have suggested, and which got canonized in the 'fundamental theorems of welfare economics' (e.g. Mas-Colell et al., 1995: chap. 10). Real markets can be very different: for example, they can fail to reach an equilibrium because there is a monopoly, because they create 'externalities' (effects on third parties for which no price is being paid), or because participants do not have full information about the goods and services in question. Economists describe such situations as 'market failures', and have analysed various ways in which they can be corrected (e.g. by putting taxes on negative externalities or providing subsidies for positive ones). This terminology is slightly misleading, however, in the sense that it suggests that such failures are an exception to the rule. Arguably, market failures of different kinds are ubiquitous, and not all of them can easily be fixed by policy measures such as taxation (see also Heath, 2014). In fact, many arguments *against* markets, brought forward by their critics, have to do with the fact that many markets do *not* sufficiently resemble the simplistic models of perfectly competitive markets in undergraduate textbooks.

How do the three traditions I had distinguished earlier look at markets? The liberal-egalitarian tradition is probably most positive towards them, picking up arguments from economists about markets providing more freedoms than other, more coercive mechanisms for coordinating economic activities (e.g. Thomas, 2017). If markets are competitive, individuals have choices: as sovereign consumers, they can choose what to buy, as workers, they can choose between different employers, and so on. Moreover, markets – at least fully competitive ones – force companies, through price competition, to offer products and services to customers at the lowest possible price. High profits should, according to textbook logic, only come about as the result of *innovation*, the benefits of which can spread to all members of society. Thus, even though they may create inequality, markets seem to fit well into the Rawlsian framework: they offer certain freedoms, and the difference principle might be understood as justifying them directly if the least-off members of society benefit from them. This reading of Rawls, however, has been rightly criticized as too simple (see e.g. Reiff, 2012), and Rawls himself also referred to institutions other than markets for ensuring a social minimum (Rawls, 1999, section 43).

It is important here to note a key difference between classical liberals (Smith, Ricardo, Hayek, etc.) and what Freeman (2011) called 'high liberals' (Mill, Dewey, Rawls, etc.). Classical liberals put great emphasis on individual property rights and see markets as flowing from the fact that individuals have the right to do whatever they like with their property, which includes buying and selling it. From this perspective, individuals have no responsibility to think of the effects on others when making decisions about their property rights, as long they do not violate anyone's rights; states should interfere with property rights as little as possible. High liberals do not give so much weight to individual property rights. Instead, they see them as an instrument for bringing about good outcomes, for example, an efficient allocation of goods and services, which can increase the freedoms and capabilities of all members of society (see also Sen, 1985). Markets are justified, on that reading, not because they flow from individual property rights but because making them part of the economic system brings about good results. This also implies that if markets *fail* to deliver good results, they should be restructured or abolished; for example, markets might not be an effective instrument when it comes to providing specific goods such as healthcare or education.

From this 'high liberal' perspective, redistributive taxation also has a different character than from the classical liberal one. For classical liberals, it is an interference with individual rights that must meet high demands of justification, whereas for 'high liberals', it is simply one instrument, among many others, for designing an economic system that realizes, as well as possible, the demands of justice (Murphy and Nagel, 2002). Moreover, from the perspective of high liberalism, the many *different* forms that markets can take deserve attention: some might have freedom-enhancing and distributively just outcomes, others not. The task of governments, on that view, is to design markets in ways that make the best possible use of them, from the perspective of justice. This might, for example, mean admitting them for goods that are can be regulated relatively easily and for which consumers really know best what their own preferences are – but not necessarily to rely on markets when the goods in questions are more difficult to evaluate and when there can be perverse incentives for suppliers, as in markets for health products.

From a neo-republican perspective, markets were initially seen in a positive light, similar to the liberal-egalitarian perspective (e.g. Pettit, 2006). After all, competitive markets can be an institutional tool for preventing one-sided domination (e.g. Anderson, 2017, chap. I). Whereas a feudal lord can impose his arbitrary will on his serfs, employers in a competitive labour market need to take into account the fact that that employees might change jobs, which reduces the power they have over them. The 'exit option' (Hirschman, 1970) in competitive markets thus has an anti-domination function, while the competition between actors on the same side of the market keeps their power in check.

But this positive picture has been criticized within the neo-republican camp, and more recent approaches are often more critical of markets. These authors point out that many forms of domination can exist in markets and through markets. For example, in labour markets employees often have to accept the conditions set by employers, which can be exploitative, extracting more value from workers than would be possible in egalitarian work relations (Vrousalis, 2023). This has led some neo-republicans to raise questions about workers' counterpower (Gourevitch, 2018). There are also forms of domination that can arise at a structural level when economic relations are organized through markets. For example, capital owners can be understood as dominating the rest of society because they can threaten to withdraw their capital, thereby harming the rest of society (if such a withdrawal is legally allowed, that is; for a discussion see also Bennett, 2021). Moreover, in international financial relations, the economic power of some countries allows them to unilaterally impose their will on others, for example, when it comes to monetary policy, because international trade takes place in their currencies (Herzog, 2021).

In critical theory and socialist thought, the attitude towards markets tends to be even less positive. In addition to forms of critique that build on norms of justice – for example, critiques of the exploitation of workers – one also finds critiques that emphasize the *alienation* that capitalist economic institutions, including markets, create (e.g. Jaeggi, 2016). In labour markets, it is argued, individuals are separated from the fruits of their labour and their own acts of production ('self-estrangement'), but also from the human species as part of biological nature, and from their fellow workers, with whom they stand in relations of competition (Marx 1844/2000). Moreover, marketization leads to shallow, instrumental relations among individuals, which undermines the solidarity that they should have as fellow citizens (Hussain, 2020). So-called 'market socialists' (e.g. Bardhan and Roemer, 1993; Schweickart, 2011) nonetheless think that socialists should accept markets for their beneficial outcomes, especially for the way in which they can facilitate efficient allocations. Therefore, markets can and should be integrated into economic systems that are otherwise organized in non-capitalist ways and aims at far greater equality than we currently see (see also Carens, 1981).

Other theorists in this tradition are more sceptical about the role of markets, pointing out their tendency to expand into ever more spheres of life and to extract value from them (e.g. Fraser, 2023). Therefore, markets should play only a very limited role: they should determine neither the distribution of basic goods and services, nor allow for the private appropriation of the social surplus, to produce high levels of private wealth. If markets were used only for the middle spectrum of the socio-economic distribution and for non-essential goods – while the high inequality they can create would be prevented (e.g. through taxation) and poorer members of society would receive support for all essential provisions – their character would be quite different (Fraser, 2023: 154–156).

What, then, does it mean to 'tame' markets? While the specific arguments differ between the three approaches, they all agree that there are areas of life that should *not* be determined by market forces. Within the liberal-egalitarian camp there is an explicit discussion about 'moral limits of markets': about goods that should *not* be traded for money, that is, not be 'commodified' (e.g. Bertrand and

Panitch, 2024). Typical candidates for such a discussion are sex work or surrogate motherhood. While defenders of markets in such goods point to the potential for mutual welfare improvements, critics emphasize the risks of one-sided dependence or exploitation. Satz (2010, chap. 4) provides four parameters for evaluating which goods should not be traded in markets, because these markets would become 'toxic': extremely harmful outcomes for individuals, extremely harmful outcomes for society, very weak or highly asymmetric knowledge or agency, and extreme vulnerabilities. For example, advertisement for unhealthy food items directed at children is problematic, because it can produce extremely harmful outcomes (a trajectory of lifelong obesity), and children have weak agency and are extremely vulnerable. What Satz focuses on, as basic normative principle, is the equal moral standing of citizens, which is undermined in toxic market relations.

Other arguments turn around the social meaning of goods, which might be changed or undermined by them being traded in markets (e.g. Sandel, 2012: 9). Against these types of arguments, Brennan and Jaworski (2015) have argued that social meanings are not set in stone and might change. Such change might be worthwhile if there is a potential for welfare gains, as had historically happened with markets for life insurance (ibid.). But arguably, in many cases, what is at stake is not *only* social meaning, but also one or more of the risks that Satz (2010) discusses.

While the liberal-egalitarian tradition thus provides arguments for limiting certain markets, the neo-republican and socialist traditions raise additional questions about domination and other harmful effects, which might provide additional reasons for limiting the sphere of markets in society. There can also be problematic *indirect* effects of markets, resulting from the overall distribution of market and non-market spheres in society. One important question, in this context, concerns the effects of markets on social cohesion and solidarity among citizens. While markets can allow for reciprocal relations between suppliers and customers (Bruni and Sugden, 2008), they pitch those people against each other who stand on the same side of the market, for example, two families who both want to rent an apartment in the housing market, which can undermine solidarity (Hussain, 2020). If citizens do not feel any solidarity among each other, it can become more difficult for them to hold those with economic or political power to account. From a perspective of non-domination, it is crucial not to let markets undermine the very conditions of the possibility of taming them.

Power relations are also crucial for another way – in addition to keeping them out of certain areas of society – in which markets can be 'tamed': to push them into a certain direction, for example towards investments in green energy rather than fossil fuels. This can, in principle, be done in various ways: governments can ban new investments in fossil fuels, or put prohibitively high taxes on their sale, while subsidizing investments in green energy. There can also be strategies via courts: citizens or civil society organizations can take corporations to court to limit the harms they do to the environment and to current and future generations. Other approaches include demonstrations, letters to parliamentarians, contributions to public discourse, or boycotts (e.g. Beck, 2018; Berkey, 2021). Such additional measures can keep the topic on the political agenda and thereby increase the pressure on economic actors.

On all these levels, however, economic actors also use their power to work *against* such 'taming' of markets. This can happen through corporate lobbying (e.g. Parvin, 2022), but also through strategies that use 'passive power', such as threatening to cut jobs, or through attempts to keep topics off the agenda, or to influence the preferences and beliefs of citizens through biased information. All three 'faces' of power that Lukes (1974/2005) had described thus play a role in the struggles around the 'taming' of markets. A key question, therefore, is whether a society, through its democratic practices, is indeed in a position 'to impose its will' on economic actors. As mentioned earlier, in the social-democratic tradition, this ideal has been described as the 'primacy of politics' (Berman, 2006).

Today, there are serious questions about the ability of democratic politics to shape markets in this way. Different democratic countries have different rules about institutional issues such as campaign finance, which influence the degree to which money plays a role in politics. And yet, it is clear that in many countries, there is a huge imbalance between the political influence of rich organizations and individuals, and average citizens (e.g. Cagé, 2020; Bagg, 2024). The greater the socio-economic inequality, and the greater the economic power of corporations, especially transnational ones, the more precarious the 'primacy of policy' becomes (White, 2011; Christiano, 2012). Money not only buys lobbyists and PR agents but also better lawyers, influence on academic institutions, attention on (social) media, and other forms of social influence. From the perspective of critical theorists and socialists, therefore, more massive reforms of the current system are needed to establish true democracy. A key question in these discussions is the role of property rights, to which I therefore turn next.

2.2 The Role of Property Rights

The socialist tradition holds that true changes in social structures can only come about if not only laws, regulations, and social norms but also property rights change. More concretely, a key proposal is that the 'means of production' need to be socialized, in the sense that it is no longer a small group of capital owners but society as a whole that determines how to organize production and consumption. This can be understood as an argument about power: property rights in the means of production are the root cause of capitalists' power over workers; hence, this is where change needs to happen. Changes at the level of the 'superstructure' (laws, public norms, etc.) can only be effective if accompanied by changes in property rights.

This argument has often been met with resistance, especially from the classical liberal and libertarian camp. The abolition of private property, commentators warned, would undermine personal freedom (e.g. Nozick, 1974). Economic regulation and the public organization of certain areas of the economy, for example, the health system, would lead society onto a 'road to serfdom', as Hayek (1944) had famously put it. There is also the fear that publicly owned resources would suffer from the 'tragedy of the commons', that is, overuse and neglect resulting from private interests and insufficient care for the long-term sustenance of common goods (Hardin, 1968). Private property, so this argument goes, makes individual owners take responsibility for the maintenance and protection of their assets. From that perspective, many of the problems of today's economic systems – especially the enormous environmental harms they cause – have to do with a *lack* of property rights: what is needed are *more* property rights, for example (tradeable) rights to emit CO_2.

This debate, which divides defenders of socialism from defenders of capitalism, has often been very polemical, especially in the Cold War era.[9] It is helpful to draw a few conceptual distinctions in order to pin down where the disagreements lie and which positions are most defensible. A first distinction is between personal property and productive property (e.g. Rawls, 2001: 138). While antisocialist rhetoric sometimes suggests the opposite, the focus of the debate about property rights and economic power needs to be on productive property. Personal property, in the sense of personal items that do not play a role in the production process (family albums, private furniture, maybe also private homes) can stay in the hands of private individuals, at least up to a point. There are also third forms, for example, local public goods, that fall between personal and productive property. As empirical research by Elinor Ostrom and others has shown (e.g. Ostrom, 1990), it is well possible for such 'commons' to be governed effectively by local communities. While they can provide alternatives to certain forms of private property, however, they are also not at the core

---

[9] It was also, in part, fuelled by the financing of pro-market thinkers and organizations by private corporations; see e.g. Burgin, 2012.

of the discussion about property rights in productive assets, because many of the latter do not have the structure of commons.

Property rights are best understood as a bundle of different rights (e.g. Grey, 1980; Gaus, 2012, but for an opposing view see, e.g., Narveson, 2010). Honoré has famously distinguished eleven key 'incidents' of property: 'the right to possess, the right to use, the right to manage, the right to the income of the things, the right to the capital, the right to security, the right or incidents of transmissibility and absence of term, the prohibition of harmful use, liability to execution, and the incident of residuarity' (1961: 113). None of these incidents needs to be absolute. For example, the right of possession, which includes the control of goods and the exclusion of others, can, in the case of property in land, be combined with a public right to trespass (ibid.: 115); the right to security is compatible with a public right to expropriate with adequate compensation (ibid.: 119).

Understanding property rights as bundles of rights opens up the possibility of moving the debate beyond the unhelpful dichotomy in which the only two alternatives are absolute private property rights or absolute public ownership. In principle, property rights are very flexible instruments and can be designed in many different ways, depending on the goods at stake and their functions in society. One can, for example, imagine that a group of people has a joint right to possess and use a property, secured over a long period of time, without having rights to capital or to destroy the asset. The incident of 'prohibition of harmful use' is particularly important: it shows that there is no need for a new, additional argument for measures such as banning CO_2 emissions, but that the prohibition of harm has always been a dimension of property. Governments can thus design different bundles of productive property rights, in the ways that allow them to best achieve their goals, for example, to increase public welfare.[10] While public ownership in the way in which it was historically practiced in the USSR has, for good reasons, a bad reputation, this does not mean that there could not be other forms in which public ownership rights could be carved out, to prevent waste and negligence and to contribute to the public good.

An important incident, when it comes to questions about economic power, is the 'right to manage'. It is often assumed that the 'right to manage' flows directly from the ownership in productive assets, for example, if the owner of a farm gives commands to the labourers working on the fields. But already early in the twentieth century, legal scholars commented on the fact that the

---

[10] This is a view of property rights in productive assets that sees them as products of government, not as natural rights that would logically precede government. In the history of political thought, this view is associated with Hobbes, while a pre-government view is associated with Locke, and also endorsed by many classical liberal and libertarian thinkers.

management of firms had gone over to the hands of managers. The latter act in the interest of owners, but it is not clear how well owners can control them (e.g., Berle and Means, 1932). Against the mainstream view that often simply assumes that there is a direct line of justification from ownership to delegation to the 'right to manage', McMahon (2012) has recently argued that the right to command over workers cannot be derived from ownership. Instead, it needs to be derived from the creation of a public legal structure – such as the corporation – that is set up by governments in order to allow for the efficient coordination of work. From this perspective, the power over companies, and hence also over workers, need not, or not exclusively, lie with owners.

What adds to the problem is that legally speaking, shareholders do not own 'the corporation'. Rather, they own the shares, and the corporation is a legal entity of its own, with its own property, separated from the private property of the shareholders, and with limited liability (e.g. Ciepley, 2013). The rights of owners to do 'whatever they want' with their property is often justified by pointing to the fact that they are liable for their property. Shareholders, however, are only liable for their investments in shares; their other assets cannot be touched if a corporation they have invested in goes bankrupt. This raises questions about the degree to which shareholder ownership should imply, even only indirectly, a 'right to manage'. Questions about the power of shareholders in today's societies are made even more complex by the fact that shareholders are often not private individuals, but large funds, for example, pension funds, whose managers can amass enormous power (e.g. Christophers 2023). Many of them operate as index funds; that is, they do not have an active investment strategy but follow general market trends, which can create a power vacuum with regard to corporations (Rothstein, 2021).

Nonetheless, when it comes to *societal* power, corporations are major players. Even though this power may not be based on property rights alone, there is a noteworthy asymmetry: corporations typically rely on formal property rights, for example, by buying up land for their operations. Other players in society, for example, local populations or environmental NGOs, often need to operate with other means, if only for lack of funds. They can, for example, try to publicly shame a corporation that pollutes the environment, or they can try to organize other players, for example, consumers, into a boycott (e.g. Beck, 2018; Berkey, 2021). But they often do not have rights comparable in strength to property rights, for example, rights in a clean environment that would be *enforceable as property rights*. Moreover, in many societies property rights enjoy a high degree of public support, maybe because individuals fear that if they are challenged, their *own* property might also be at risk (even though the distinction between personal and productive property makes clear that the discussion is *not* about personal property). This often creates a default assumption in favour of those with property rights, putting the burden of proof on those who want to limit or redesign them for the sake of other goods.

But this is no necessary implication of the notion of property rights, especially those in productive assets – they could also be seen, in a much more flexible way, as tools for shifting the economy in a direction that serves the common good. From this perspective, one could repair the asymmetry between property rights and other (environmental, social, etc.) concerns either by weakening property rights in productive assets and putting stricter limitations on what can be done with such property, or by creating new property rights in order to protect other goods. The latter strategy has been tried by, for example, by giving legal status to environmental entities, such as rivers, which then have rights that can stand up against the property rights of corporations or other economic actors. However, critics have questioned whether this is the right way forward, because it continues the logic of private property rights, instead of orienting the economic system towards other principles (e.g. Martinez-Alier, 2002).

But either of these strategies presupposes that those with property rights in productive assets are not already so powerful that changing the property regime in such ways in doomed to fail from the start. If the latter is the case, a society is, at its core, no longer democratic: the 'demos' can no longer govern itself, because those who own the means of production have too much power. Whether or not that is the case depends, crucially, on the question of what *political* power comes with property rights in productive assets. And as the discussion of the three faces of power, described on p. 14–15 above, makes clear, this is not only a question about political proposals that get put on the table and then accepted or rejected. It also concerns proposals that are *not* put on the agenda, and the way in which powerful actors influence the preferences and beliefs of other players, so that they cannot even imagine alternatives to the status quo.

At least two parameters determine the strength of the political power that property rights in productive assets bring – and this concerns not only property in productive assets but also high amounts of private property *tout court,* for example, inherited wealth (note, though, such wealth would typically come from ownership in productive assets by previous generations). A first is the concentration of ownership: if these property rights are concentrated among a small group, while the rest of society depends, in some way or another, on access to the property in question, then this obviously gives the former group greater power. If property is dispersed, in contrast, any single owner cannot have so much influence, because those who need access to a certain type of property have alternative options. This is the basic mechanism behind the intuition that a competitive economy, with lots of small owners, is less dangerous for the primacy of politics than one in which economic power is highly concentrated. At the beginning of the twentieth century, this was one of the motivations behind strong anti-trust legislation in the United States, which led to the breaking up of several 'trusts'. But this perspective on anti-trust lost influence, in the second half of the twentieth century, when only the impact of market concentration on consumer prices, instead of considerations about power, came to determine the thinking about anti-trust legislation (Khan, 2017).

A similar intuition – that decentralized property rights pose a lesser risk to democratic politics – also accompanies the discussions about a 'property-owning democracy', in which the ownership in the means of production is meant to be widely dispersed among the population (Bagg, 2024: 225–229). In such an economic system, all individuals would be at once capitalists and workers, overcoming the structural conflict between capital and labour (Thomas, 2017). Note, however, that even dispersed owners can exert undue political influence if their interests are clustered, for example, when small business owners come together in associations, or when widespread ownership of shares is concentrated in pension funds (see also O'Neill, 2020b). In such cases, the managers of such associations or funds can have great political power, for example, through lobbying *on behalf of their members*.

A second parameter that determines how much political power comes with property rights has to do with *what one is allowed to do* with property, especially with money. Here, the discussion about the limits of markets comes back. For example, it is clear that unregulated campaign finances give rich organizations and individuals more possibilities to influence politics. Take the controversial 2010 Supreme Court judgement 'Citizen United' in the United States: it lifted all restrictions on private money to flow into so-called 'Super PACs' to support political candidates or causes. In other democratic countries, there are stricter rules on political donations, and campaigns are at least partly publicly financed, limiting this kind of influence of money on politics. But the 'market' in political influence is just one of the relevant markets through which money can buy power in society. Another example is legal representation: the legal system can only function fairly for all members of society if they all have access to good legal representation. In today's societies, those with more money can pay for better lawyers, often pressuring those with fewer financial means into out-of-court settlements that work to their disadvantage (if they dare to take a conflict to court at all). Some commentators (e.g. Agmon, 2021) therefore argue for a ban on the marketization of legal representation. If legal representation is a commodity in markets, those with greater resources, for example, corporations, can acquire more (or higher quality) of it, undercutting the functioning of an adversarial legal system in which all parties need to have at least adequate legal representation. Therefore, those unable to pay for legal representation should be provided with it by the state, and there might also be a ceiling on how much richer parties are allowed to spend on legal representation.

If such restrictions, and many others that would be needed to reinstall and stabilize the 'primacy of politics', can be imposed on private property rights in productive assets, then the case for abolishing these private property rights becomes less urgent. But whether this is possible depends, in turn, on the very power of those with property rights in productive assets: Do they have to accept such regulations, or can they successfully lobby against them, or thwart them in other ways? This circularity is indeed a typical feature of the way in which power functions: different forms of power often reinforce and stabilize each other (Claassen and Herzog, 2021). If economic power has grown beyond a certain point, it feeds more political power, and vice versa. Then the power of wealthy elites becomes too entrenched to impose political regulation onto them. In such a situation, the only way to break through this self-reinforcing cycle may indeed be to challenge the very distribution of property rights in productive assets.

One possible reaction to this situation is to call for an upper limit of wealth (of whatever kind) – an argument for which Robeyns (2022) uses the term 'limitarianism'. An argument for limitarianism can be made on the basis of considerations of justice: it is simply unjust that so many poor members of society have basic needs unmet, while others live in luxury. Maybe even stronger, however, is the argument from democracy: it is impossible to have a stable democracy, in the long term, if material inequality becomes too large. In addition to the self-reinforcing cycles of economic and political power, there is also the sociological problem of class formation: a highly unequal society will almost inevitably develop class structures (Herzog, 2024b). The members of different classes will then not any longer see each other as equal co-governors of their common affairs. Democratic societies cannot let this happen, and should therefore work on the breaking up of concentrated wealth. For democracy to flourish – and to remain stable over time – it is crucial that material inequalities do not go unchecked, so that citizens can continue to see each other as moral equals.

And yet, in the current situation it seems unduly reductionist (and pessimistic) to see a redistribution of property rights as the *only* possible lever – while it is an essential one, others can and should also be moved. Political power *can* still impose certain rules on corporations and rich individuals. This is especially likely to be successful at the transnational level: the European Union has regularly imposed rules on transnational corporations, for example, with regard to data privacy, and these regulations were then often taken over by other countries (Bradford, 2020). This indicates that not everything is lost when it comes to the 'primacy of politics'. But the power of democratic politics is still precarious, especially in countries that have endorsed the belief in free markets and a 'small state'. Therefore, reforms are urgently needed to reaffirm democratic political power against the holders of private property. Whether a complete abolition of private property in the means of production is needed, or whether other forms of reasserting democratic power over the economy are also possible, will show itself in the process.

2.3 Democracy and the Economy

The two previous sections have shown that the relation between economic and political power in many societies is unbalanced. While markets can, in principle, be beneficial social institutions, at least if they are regulated well and applied only to goods for which they are suitable, many markets that we see today have not been appropriately tamed. The property rights of many economic actors are not designed in ways that serve the interests of society as a whole; sometimes they even work *against* the latter, as when property rights are taken to include a permission to harm the environment. As mentioned on p. 25 above, there is an asymmetry between how different societally important goals are regulated, namely, to have a well-functioning economy and to also achieve various social goals and to protect the environment. The former is done by means of property rights – which are typically very strong rights – in the means of production; the latter is typically done through other legal means, for example regulations, taxes or subsidies. This asymmetry in strength gives economic actors over-proportionate means for protecting their interests. This contributes to the harm currently done to the environment, the climate, and thereby also to many individuals, now and in the future. And the concentration of private economic power, especially in the form of property rights in the means of production, raises questions about the very possibility of political regulation against these powerful interests.

These are fundamental challenges for the model I have presented so far, in which democratic politics 'sets the frame' for economic practices, including markets, and otherwise lets them follow their own dynamics. Especially in the post-World War II era, it was often assumed that there is a kind of three-part division of labour between politics and the economy: politics sets the fundamental frame, by securing property and providing public goods such as security. Then, economic actors take over, in the 'private economy' in which markets ensure efficient outcomes and economic growth. This leads to a bigger 'economic pie' than other approaches, for example, a planned economy, would be able to deliver (and 'market economies' were also seen as more compatible with individual freedom, see, e.g., Ciepley, 2007). Governments then, in a third step, tax the ensuing profits, to pay for public services and to redistribute some income to those who are not successful in the economy, for example, the unemployed.

But this model only makes sense if governments *can* indeed set the frame for the economy, also against private interests – and as I have argued, today, there are reasons to be sceptical about this. An additional reason for questioning this model is that the third step, the taxation of profits, has also been hollowed out in recent decades. International corporations, but also rich private individuals and families, use numerous gaps in international tax regulations to avoid paying taxes. For example, they shift profits to countries with low taxation, even though no economic activity takes place there (Dietsch, 2015). This has undermined the capacity of many governments to provide public services and welfare state institutions that ensure a life in dignity for all members of society. Again, this is an issue of power: Are democratic governments able to impose taxation on international corporations or individuals, or do they cave in whenever the latter threaten to remove capital from a country, or to stop supporting political candidates? Here, international collaboration between governments is obviously needed, so that corporations can no longer play them out against each other.

Instead of only trying to fix this old model, to really redress the current imbalance of power between democratic politics and the economy, I suggest another model: to imbed democratic values *in the economy itself* (e.g. Cumbers, 2020; Herzog, 2025). The normative basis for this model are the principles of democracy, together with a social scientific hypothesis about how these principles can be realized and stabilized in the long term. The basic argument is this:

1) Democracy as political system is normatively justified (this can be done on the basis of more fundamental principles, for example the equal moral status of all members of society).
2) For democracy to be stably realized in institutions and practices, its principles must be part of the everyday experience of citizen, where they can get reinforced and deepened.
3) A large part of the everyday experience of citizens takes place in economic institutions and practices (and it is legitimate to shape these through public policy).
4) Therefore, democratic principles need to be embedded in economic institutions and practices, in order to stably realize democracy.

In the old model, the prime value embedded in the economy was efficiency (at least this was the official narrative, which arguably often served as a smokescreen for greed, brute and simple). But efficiency is not itself a first order value; rather, it concerns the question of how to achieve first order values *in the way that best avoids the waste of resources*. As LeGrand (1990) has argued, one often finds a rhetoric that suggests an inevitable trade-off between efficiency and other values, for example, equality or justice. But this framing is misguided. Economic policy certainly often involves trade-offs of first-order values, for example, between individual rights and the public good. These trade-offs need to be decided by fair democratic processes in which all members of society have a voice, with the legal system providing additional checks, for example, to protect minority rights. Only then, in a logically second step, comes the question of how to achieve the point on the trade-off one has democratically opted for *in the most efficient way*. Efficiency, and also economic growth to which it is often connected, are insufficiently specific as normative criteria: many possible states of the economy, with very different distributions, can be efficient or can lead to growth. Therefore, one always has to ask: efficiency for whom, or growth for whom?

What does it mean to instead embed democratic values in the economy, as suggested by the argument on p. 29 above? A key imperative, for formal and informal institutions alike, is that they do not undermine the basic mutual respect that the citizens of a democracy owe to each other as moral equals. This means that certain forms of economic behaviour, which a pure focus on efficiency might not register as problematic, must not be allowed to happen.

Let me make this more concrete with regard to markets (in the next section, I will discuss what it means for the organization of work). Embedding democratic values in markets means more than taming them in the sense of keeping them out of certain societal spheres or pushing them into socially desirable directions, for example, towards renewable energy, although these points remain important. In addition, they must be designed such that genuine win-win outcomes with a fair distribution of the benefits can arise. This means that market transactions that involve deception, or that take advantage of the weakness of will of other market participants, are not legitimate (in fact, from an efficiency-perspective, they would sometimes not be permissible either, because the market participants do not have sufficient information or do not act on the basis of their own well-considered preferences). Moreover, markets with one-sided market power, in which the benefits go mostly or fully to one side, need to be avoided. For even if all participants enter certain markets seemingly voluntarily – because they have no alternative – markets can be exploitative. Different theories of exploitation, from the liberal-egalitarian, neo-republican and socialist camp, define it differently, but they would agree on many real-life cases in today's societies, for example, low-wage labour, being in fact exploitative (see, e.g., Reiff, 2013 for a liberal view of exploitation, or Vrousalis, 2023 for a socialist account that also draws on republican elements).

One way of preventing such exploitative situations is by providing a public alternative that creates a minimum floor for all market transactions. A public job guarantee at a living wage, for example, provides all those who need to work for an income with an alternative to employment in private businesses (Tcherneva, 2020). Public housing opportunities provide an alternative to rented or privately owned housing, and thereby also create a minimum floor. Public banking options protect individuals from having to resort to payday lending with its excruciating interest rates that are often the cause of a downward spiral into personal bankruptcy (Baradaran, 2015). Such measures can ensure that the most vulnerable members of society are not subjected to the one-sided power of other market participants. Different countries – and also different sub-state units within countries (e.g. different states when it comes to rules for payday lending in the United States, or different municipalities when it comes to providing housing for the homeless) – differ with regard to such rules and provisions. This shows that politics has at least *some* scope for designing the rules of the game differently.

But this is not enough to prevent one-sided market power over market participants above these minimal thresholds. Many other levers can be used to bring markets *in general* better in line with democratic values. One is the direct regulation of products, for example, a ban on financial products that trick people into paying too much, or warning messages on food products that harm their health.[11] Another is the regulation of the information that must be provided about products, both concerning its content and its form of presentation, to make sure that customers do not fall prey to misleading information. A third point is that in so far as markets *are* justifiable for certain goods or services, politics needs to ensure there is real competition, so that consumers have a true choice between suppliers. Many markets that we see today are highly concentrated and this creates one-sided power, to the disadvantage of customers (e.g. Philippon,

---

[11] It might be objected that this creates a risk of paternalism: Why shouldn't people be allowed to consume harmful products? In response, several points can be made. First, some products can create such massive and irreversible harms (e.g. immediate death or severe health damage) that paternalism is indeed justified. Second, in less harmful cases (or cases in which moderate consumption might be justified despite some harm in the long run), consumers should be allowed to make their own choices, but on a good informational basis, rather than being nudged along by the companies offering such products. The government might want to counter such commercial nudges by transparent provision of information or warning signs (for a discussion see Schmidt, 2017).

2019 on the United States). It is, once again, a matter of the 'primacy of politics' to make sure that public anti-trust authorities are sufficiently powerful to prevent market concentration.

Last but not least, in many markets, counterpower organizations can help to redress what would otherwise be massive power imbalances (see also Bagg, 2024). Take labour markets: typically, employers have more power, because employees depend more on their income than employers depend on any individual worker. But this can be different if workers can form unions: if they stand together as a group, the balance of power vis-à-vis employers is very different (they may still be at a disadvantage, however, if employers can threaten to move jobs abroad). Historically, the role of unions was crucial, in many countries, for making gains for workers. Without unions and their core instrument, strikes, work time reduction – for example, the famous campaign for an eight-hour workday – would probably never have happened (e.g. Alesina et al., 2005). But at least since the 1980s, unions have been weakened, not only by market-friendly governments but also by a whole industry of union-busting legal advisors, paid for by companies. Organizations of counter-power in other markets, for example renter associations, have also been weakened. Rebuilding such organizations is crucial, and politics can support these processes, for example, by facilitating the setting up of such organizations, or by mandating industry-wide, instead of company-wide, collective bargaining (see also Block and Sachs, 2020).

In addition to changes in formal institutions, there are also questions about the informal social norms – the culture – that a democracy needs, and how the economic system influences them. The latter should, at a minimum, not undermine or erode a democratic culture, and, ideally, support it. These informal norms are more difficult to grasp than formal rules, and political philosophy has often neglected them. One might argue that formal institutions are ultimately more important: they are backed up by the coercive power of the state, after all, which is also why their legitimation requires particular attention. But human beings do not only react to coercive power. Other forms of power function via social norms, which are backed up by, for example, the possibility of losing approval from one's peers or of being socially excluded. If one assumes, as philosophers from Rousseau to Honneth have done (see Iser, 2019 for an overview), that human beings are creatures who seek the recognition of others, then it is clear that social norms can have a powerful influence on human behaviour as well.

One area that illustrates this point well is justice with regard to gender, race, sexual orientation, age, health, and other demographic features. In most Western democracies, there are legal rules that forbid discrimination along these lines, embedding the democratic imperative to treat all individuals equally, for example, in labour markets. And yet, many differences remain in place; these can be seen, for example, in the absence of people of colour or other minorities in positions of power, even in organizations that have publicly committed themselves to diversity. These differences are not only distributively unjust but also expose some groups to the risk of being dominated and exploited by others – and the more disadvantages intersect, the more vulnerable individuals typically are, in specific ways (a phenomenon captured by theories of 'intersectionality', see e.g. Crenshaw, 1989).

Philosophers have discussed questions about discrimination and disadvantages, for example, in discussions about 'structural injustice' (Young, 2011) or about 'epistemic injustice', the injustice of treating people unequally, on the basis of irrelevant demographic features, in their status as bearers of knowledge (Fricker, 2007; Kidd and Medina, 2017). But these discussions have not yet been sufficiently integrated with questions about *economic* justice, even though the economy is one of the areas where these forms of injustice often play out and have drastic effects. For example, discrimination that individuals experience along lines of gender, race, or health status often takes place within the economic realm, with further harmful consequences. If individuals from certain groups do not dare to speak up in the workplace, for example – or they do dare to speak up, but are not taken seriously by others – their material interests are also likely to be unfairly neglected compared to the interests of others.

Here is an example of how economic issues intersect with questions about a democratic culture without discrimination. The public space of many Western democracies is, to a considerable extent, dominated by commercial speech, in the form of advertising. Different countries have different norms about the extent of truthfulness in advertisement; in the United States, for example, the concept of 'puffery' allows for many untrue statements, on the assumption that individuals would not believe them anyway (even though empirical research shows that they often do, see Hoffman, 2006 for an overview). One can, of course, evaluate the regulation of advertisement on the basis of economic criteria such as efficiency, or on the basis of broader criteria, such as justice. But one can – and in my view, one should – also ask whether the norms of public speech that are expressed in advertisement are compatible with democratic values. It is, after all, likely that from the perspective of the audience, 'public speech' is not separated into political speech, on the one hand, and economic speech, on the other. If one assumes that these forms of speech, *together*, influence the perception and practice of social norms, and that democracy needs these norms to be shaped in a certain way – for example, avoiding discrimination – then this raises questions about what kind of advertisement regulation democratic societies should give themselves.

Of course, such regulation can be in tension with freedom of speech, which is also a crucial value and essential for democracy (e.g. Shiffrin, 2014). But arguably, freedom of speech matters mostly *for individuals as citizens*, not so much for commercial organization whose speech is motivated by the goal of making profits. It therefore does not seem to be too much of a restriction of the rights of corporations to ban untruthful and misleading speech in advertisement that might harm consumers, especially vulnerable ones such as children. It is also in line with democratic norms to expect companies not to undermine the democratic value of respect for all members of society, for example, by not portraying women in objectifying ways that deny them this respect. Interestingly, there are often public outcries when such violations happen, and companies then sometimes change their strategies on their own. This indicates that social norms can play a role even vis-à-vis these powerful players, who are afraid of damaging their reputation.

A last dimension of embedding democratic values in the economy has to do with overall inequality, which I have already discussed in relation to property rights. The larger socio-economic inequality becomes, the more difficult it becomes to keep up democratic principles and a democratic culture. The risks of inequality are diverse. One is that it becomes more and more difficult to keep money from spilling into spheres where it should not play a role (Walzer, 1983). I had already mentioned the problem of campaign finances and other direct flows of money from rich individuals to political actors, as well as problems in the legal system, in which the playing field become more and more uneven if richer individuals and organizations can buy better legal representation. In addition, there is the whole area of health: access to healthcare and a healthy lifestyle should not depend on one's finances, and yet this is the case in many countries, in deep tension with their democratic values. Education is another case: in a democratic society, children from all backgrounds should get a good education and be able to enter any career that fits their talents and interests. But this kind of equality of opportunity does not exist, and it has in fact declined over the last decades, hand in hand with growing inequality (e.g. Chetty, 2018).

How can inequality be reduced? There are numerous policy suggestions for redistributing unequal wealth, for example, an inheritance tax, redistribution of capital towards individuals from poorer families (e.g. in the form of a capital grant that gets paid at the eighteenth birthday and that can be used for purposes such as education, housing or starting a business) (e.g. Atkinson, 2015; Piketty, 2020). In the case of inheritance, the normative case for redistribution is particularly strong, because children have done nothing to choose their parents, so it is clearly a matter of luck, not of one's own efforts or achievements. There are also numerous other ideas about how to reduce inequality, from maximum incomes (Robeyns, 2022) to more investments in public goods, which offer the same conditions for all members of society and thus have an equalizing effect. It is not a matter of lack of ideas, or indeed good practices that have already been tried in some other country, but a matter of political will and of the power relations in a society whether such proposals are realized.

One area in which a democratic future, or a relapse into highly unequal social relations that lead to domination and exploitation, are currently very much at stake, is the organization of work. Even though we speak of labour 'markets', much work is not organized through markets, but takes place in the 'hierarchies' of large-scale organizations, whether private companies or public service institutions (Coase, 1937). Over the course of the nineteenth and twentieth century, many Western societies had fought for improvements of workers' rights and working conditions, together with the fight for democratic rights. They have also fought, with mixed success in different countries, for democratic rights *within* companies. But in the last decades, these rights have, in many countries, been weakened and rolled back, creating forms of work that are hardly compatible with democratic values. In the next section, I turn to this issue and discuss it in more detail.

3 Work between Politics and Economics

How should a society organize the work that needs to be done to fulfil human needs? One might think that this would be a straightforward sub-question of political philosophy, in line with other questions about justice, legitimacy or democracy. And yet, in the classical canon of Western political thought, work is not a central topic. One finds ideas about the future of work, and quite radical ones, in the genre of utopian writing, suggesting, for example, a rotation of people in and out of socially necessary but unpleasant jobs in agriculture (More, 1516/1967). At least since Locke (1689/1988), work was also part of an argument about the justification of private property rights. When it comes to thinking about *politics,* however, work was, for a long time, not part of the picture. Many historical thinkers, from Greek antiquity far into the early modern period, assumed that political participation was a privilege of those who did *not* have to work, at least not in an employment relation. Those, in contrast, who had to work for a living, were not considered sufficiently independent to have a say in political matters (ancient Athenian democracy was an exception; see Meiskins Wood, 1995, chap. 7).

This changed when, over the course of the eighteenth to twentieth century, more and more groups in society, including workers, successfully fought for political rights. The question of how work should be organized was a central part of these theoretical discussions and practical political conflicts. Socialist and social-democratic parties fought *both* for the political rights of workers *and* for improvements of their working conditions and for more security, for example, through welfare systems and the public provision of services such as healthcare. In the last decades of the twentieth century, however, such discussions and political conflicts have ebbed somewhat. In the neoliberal economic vision that came to the fore in this period, labour markets were considered markets like any others, most efficiently organized if only minimally regulated.

Today, it is the arrival and spread of new technologies such as artificial intelligence (which can take over many more tasks than in the past) and digital communication (which allows for many forms of work to be done anywhere in the world) that raise new questions about the organization of work and its relation to politics. While some authors predict a radical reduction of work and want to work towards this goal (e.g. Danaher, 2019), there is also a risk of new forms of exploitation and vulnerability, which would let workers fall back behind everything that had been achieved in the decades- and century-long struggle of the labour movement. There has been a big discussion about 'precarization', that is, less and less secure and stable jobs, especially at the lower end of the socio-economic spectrum (e.g. Standing, 2011). Moreover, the geography and social networks of work are changing. When working on digital platforms, workers do not have a 'workplace' or 'colleagues' in the traditional sense but are instead following orders by algorithmic systems (e.g. De Stefano, 2015). When working mostly from home, the social ties between workers may also become weaker, raising question about the solidarity between them that might be needed to stand up against employers (Herzog, 2024a).

In this section, my focus will be on the relationship between work and democracy, following the argument, developed earlier, that democratic values need to be embedded within the economy itself. This is particularly relevant for work because many forms of work take place in hierarchical relationships that are in direct tension with the egalitarian values of democracy. This has led to renewed interest, in recent years, in the topic of 'workplace democracy', that is democratically organized work relations. Before moving to this topic, however, I discuss a question that has mostly been seen as a matter of *justice*, but which can also be asked from a perspective of democracy: What wage differentials are compatible with democratic values? In both cases, I will also pick up a distinction I had drawn earlier: that between ideal and non-ideal theorizing.

I conclude by connecting the topic of work to one to which it has, until now, only sparely be connected: the question of sustainability. If one assumes that our economic systems need to shift to a new equilibrium that does not transgress the planetary boundaries (Rockström et al., 2009), then a key question is what this implies for the future of work and the future of democracy.

3.1 Just Wages in a Democracy

A folk theory of wage justice, which is widespread especially in countries in which free market-thinking dominates, is that labour markets justly reward labour: what you get in the labour market is what you contribute to the creation of value, and the more you contribute, the more you get. Such a line of thinking has, with qualifications, also been endorsed by economists to justify high wage inequality (e.g. Mankiw, 2010). But it is highly questionable, for several reasons. Intuitively, many individuals find it problematic that a lot of socially necessary work, such as care for children, patients, or elderly people, receives relatively low wages (insofar as it takes the form of paid work at all), while the wages in sectors such as finance can be extremely high. The concept of 'value' at play here is obviously not a moral one, in a general sense of certain forms of work 'having value for society', but a purely financial one.

In so far as wages are determined by market forces, a crucial point to remember is that in markets, supply *and* demand determine prices, and hence also wages. Even if there is high demand for a certain type of work, in the sense that it is urgently needed for society, this does not mean that it will, in an unregulated labour market, be highly remunerated. It might not be *if there are many people who offer this kind of work,* which pushes wages down. Historically, this was one of the reasons for why, during the industrial revolution, wages were low and working conditions abysmal: there was an oversupply of labour. Similar effects can also be seen today in many areas of work that do not require specialized skills. Another case in point are industries in which many newly arrived migrants, who are in a vulnerable position and whose qualifications may not (yet) be recognized in the host country, work. The working conditions in such industries, especially those that function with very little public oversight (or even completely outside the boundaries of official labour markets), can be abysmal even today. Such work involves not only low wages and regular wage-theft, but also high risks for the health and bodily integrity of workers (e.g. Apostolidis, 2018).

Apart from this basic point about how market wages form, there are many other problems with the idea that labour markets would reward workers according to the value of their contributions. Not least among them is the problem that many real-life labour market, in contrast to abstract textbook models, are shaped by various forms of unequal power, which have an impact on the wages that form in them (for discussions, see, e.g., Manning, 2021). For example, one area of empirical research (and political controversy) is the 'gender wage gap' (e.g. Kochhar, 2023), and there is also a 'class wage gap', that is, lower average remuneration of women and individuals from lower socio-economic backgrounds (e.g. Friedman and Laurison, 2019). Empirical research can explain some of the causes of these gaps, for example, for the gender wage gap, the choice of part-time work by many women who have family responsibilities, or the fact that many industries in which the percentage of female workers is high have lower wages overall. But this does not yet provide an answer to the question of whether these differences are *justified*. The work for families that women in part-time jobs do *is* needed for social reproduction, after all. As Marxist feminists have emphasized in particular, capitalism *needs* workers to be taken care of in their homes after their working hours, and new generations of workers to be brought up (e.g. Federici, 2012). They have, therefore, provocatively asked for 'wages for housework', to draw attention to all the 'reproductive' work that makes the 'productive' work in factories or offices possible (see also Fraser, 2023, chap. 3).

What, then, might be a just distribution of wages, one that the citizens of a democratic society could justify to one another as moral equals? Here, a central discussion within the liberal-egalitarian camp deserves attention, even though it was framed in terms of justice, not democracy. With regard to distributive justice, Rawls (2001, 42–43) had famously suggested his two principles, to recall:

> "**First Principle**: Each person has the same indefeasible claim to a fully adequate scheme of equal basic liberties, which scheme is compatible with the same scheme of liberties for all;
>
> **Second Principle**: Social and economic inequalities are to satisfy two conditions:
>
> a. They are to be attached to offices and positions open to all under conditions of *fair equality of opportunity*;
> b. They are to be to the greatest benefit of the least-advantaged members of society (the *difference principle*)."

The second principle contains, next to the imperative of equal opportunities, the 'difference principle'. It has often been understood as applying to wages, as part of the economic income distribution. One reading of the principle is that if highly talented individuals can be incentivized to work hard, in the fields in which their work is most productive, then everyone in society benefits from this. High wages for jobs such as surgeons or other socially important jobs would, on that reading, be justifiable (and little discussion was dedicated to which these jobs would actually be, to the best of my knowledge).

But Cohen (e.g. 1991) raised an important objection to this argument, which he framed as a tension within Rawls' own account (see also Section 1.2 above). The assumption behind this argument is that talented individuals would *need* to be incentivized by high wages to work in the jobs in which they would contribute most to society. For example, a person with a talent for being a doctor might prefer to work as a gardener and, in that picture, require a higher wage to switch to the work of doctor. This, Cohen argued, is incompatible with another claim that Rawls also makes, namely that all members of a just society share an 'ethos of justice'. How can a talented individual share such an ethos, and yet blackmail the rest of society by threatening to withhold their talents unless they get a higher wage? Note that Cohen (1991: 313) does admit that the 'special burdens' of certain jobs, for example, the need for long training, could be compensated by somewhat higher wages. But this is not the same as allowing individuals to use their bargaining power to gain as high a salary as possible; 'special burdens' can and often do also exist in jobs in which individuals have very little bargaining power.

This discussion raised interesting questions about the relation between ideal and non-ideal theorizing. For Cohen, the difference principle has different implications to those that Rawls assumes. Treating the individual financial motives of individuals, which they might have acquired in a capitalist society but which stand in tension with an ethos of justice, as part of ideal theory, would mean to make a bad compromise with a corrupt reality, on that reading. In response, one might argue – on the side of Rawls – that the non-public nature of certain decisions – including individuals' decisions about how to behave in markets – makes them unsuitable as targets of regulation by institutions (Williams, 1998).

A related question that this discussion raised is what the 'site of justice' is (Cohen, 1997). Rawls had famously argued that justice is 'the first virtue of social institutions' (1971: 3). Individuals need to follow the norms of these institutions, for example, laws about taxation, but they need not act *out of considerations of justice* when acting as participants of the economic systems, for example, as buyers, sellers, or investors. Thus, Rawls had built his theory of justice on assumptions that resemble those of the 'primacy of politics': a division of labour between the setting of the framework (the rules of the game) and the economic activities (the moves in the game that take place within the framework). Cohen's challenge is based on the idea that justice matters all the way down, also in people's everyday interactions. This point is structurally similar to the argument, defended above (p. 29), that democratic principles should be embedded in the economic realm, in the sense that core normative principles matter not only for a certain part of the institutional structure or for a specific realm of society, but rather need to be part of people's lived experiences, also in what we call 'the economy'.

Nonetheless, one might reject this parallel by holding that for determining which wages are just, one cannot just look at the distributions that one wants to see as a just outcome. This perspective may be suspected of being too consequentialist: it looks at the *outcomes* that one wants to achieve, not at the *inputs* into the process. What, for example, about individuals who work very hard and therefore achieve a high income – should this not matter for what is distributively just? The intuition that stands behind this question is that individual *responsibility* should matter, at least to some degree, for distributive justice (e.g. Dworkin 1981a, 1981b, 2000). This point, however, leads to a follow-up question: how can one determine *which*, or *how much of a*, role individual responsibility plays in the outcomes one sees in today's (pre-tax) wage distributions?

Some theorists, for example, Malleson (2023, chap. 4–5), here take a strong position and hold that *no* outcome can be ascribed to responsibility, because all the factors that go into the make-up of different personalities, for example, their talents, how hard-working they are, how much willpower they possess, and so on, are brought about by forces outside of their own control. One's talents, just as one's physical health and one's looks, are a matter of genetics and upbringing. The 'highly talented' individuals that played a prominent role in the Rawls-Cohen-debate are not themselves responsible for their ability to create high value for society. Thus, they do not *deserve* their higher income to start with – a point on which Rawls and Cohen would probably agree, but Rawls might still admit it as an outcome of the system if the institutions of the latter, overall, promote justice.

This argument may convince some, while others may hesitate: Wouldn't it imply giving up *any* notion of responsibility, also in other contexts (e.g. criminal law), and wouldn't this undermine many of our moral practices? But one need not go so far to see that in the specific context of *labour markets*, factors other than individual responsibility play a great role (and note that in contexts such as criminal law, it takes a lot of effort to delineate individual responsibility from contextual factors, while no mechanism for making this delineation exists in labour markets). Even if one assumes that all healthy, grown-up individuals possess a basic capacity of agency, and can be held responsible for their choices, one can acknowledge that the ability to choose certain jobs is highly dependent on one's socio-economic and family background. And one can admit that it is often a matter of luck who ends up in which positions in labour markets; for example, individuals who enter their first job after university during an economic recession receive lower wages than those who enter it during an economic boom, and this effect leads to a path-dependency for future wages that can remain visible during individuals' whole working lives (e.g. Schwandt and van Wachter, 2023). One could therefore argue that while *some* differences in income may be the result of responsible choices, and thus stand in no need of correction, the differences get amplified by many factors that are not in people's hands. Redistributive taxation can then be understood as correcting for those random factors, by reducing the spread of the income distribution (Dworkin, 1981b: 313).

An additional point that underlines the role of factors outside of individual control – and which can be connected both to a framing in terms of justice, and to a framing in terms of democracy – is the way in which modern work functions through the division of labour and mutual complementarities. Value creation happens *together:* most individual jobs only make sense because they are locked into a complex system of roles that complement each other.[12] If some part of the system becomes more productive, for example, through new technologies, then all members of the system can, in principle, benefit from this. One way in which this can be seen is the fact that the same jobs can carry very different wages depending on the economy in which they are embedded and the general level of welfare and costs of living in them (e.g. Malleson, 2023: 147–148). It is not a matter of personal responsibility but of the context in which this work is done, that determines how much it pays.

It depends to a great extent on the distribution of power what the material distribution in fact looks like: which groups in society have the possibility of amassing the benefits, which ones remain disadvantaged? For example, in recent decades, from the 1980s onwards, the average wages in many Western societies have hardly risen, while the income and wealth of the top 1 per cent of society have gone up massively (e.g. Piketty, 2014). This is a matter of power: an important factor is the decline of unions, which structurally weakens labour (Stansbury and Summers, 2020). This shows, once more, how misleading it is to try to use arguments from responsibility for defending the current distribution of

---

[12] An additional problem, which I here cannot deal with for reasons of space, is that this fine-grained division of labour can lead to alienation and create physical and psychological harms to workers – topic that thinkers from Adam Smith to Marx to more recent authors (e.g. Jaeggi, 2016) have discussed. In an ideally just and democratic organization of work, measures would be taken to prevent this, e.g. through job sharing, job rotation, and the use of technologies specifically for preventing one-sided, harmful work.

wages: there are no 'neutral' market outcomes that would reflect 'only' people's contributions and nothing else. The frameworks within which markets operate are already shaped by societal power relations.

What, then, could be alternative mechanisms for achieving a wage structure that would be in line with principles of justice that equal fellow citizens could agree on? Of course, there is some scope for reasonable disagreement here: What *exactly* could be reasons for considering a job particularly burdensome, or how *exactly* should unpaid but societally necessary labour be taken into account? And yet, it seems plausible to assume that the enormous disparity of wages that we currently see in the economy – for example, in the US relations of the order of 300:1 between CEOs and average employees – is not justifiable from the perspective of *any* normative account. There are simply no plausible arguments about why this might be justifiable, whether from an individual or from a societal perspective. In fact, economists have also shown empirically that CEOs who are publicly celebrated as particularly productive are harmful to the value of companies (Malmendier and Tate, 2009) – even within a purely capitalist logic, these high levels of executive pay do not make sense.

A possible model – at the level of ideal theory – for realizing a more just and democratic distribution of wages has been suggested by Carens (1981). He argued that labour markets may well play an important role in signalling the scarcity or abundance of work in different jobs, and should therefore not be replaced by other mechanisms. Instead, their results should be rectified by massive redistribution that would go into the direction of equalizing incomes. Individuals could still be motivated to look for high-paying jobs because the pre-tax income could be a matter of social esteem for them. But they would accept that they do not, in addition to that social esteem, also deserve a higher income and would therefore be willing to have most of that income taxed away. This approach, however, presupposes that citizens have already internalized an ethos of justice – and yet are also capable of acting on two different motivational logics, pursuing high income in the market and accepting taxation afterwards – thus raising questions about the political and psychological feasibility of this proposal.

In the non-ideal here and now, more gradual steps can be taken to get labour markets somewhat closer to a justifiable distribution of wages, in line with democratic values. A first field of action is lowly-paid work, which is often done by members of disadvantaged groups. A possible instrument is a mandatory minimum wage as a living wage, expressing the fact – defended, among others, by Martin Luther King Jr. (1963/2011: 172) during the strike of sanitation workers – that 'all labor has dignity'. A second policy area concerns maximum wages, or at least prohibitively high taxation on wages that go beyond, say, ten

times the average wage. Such rules could be implemented at the level of companies or, better still, whole industries or the whole economy. It might lead to work-time reduction by talented people (unless there is a countervailing effect, namely that they will have to work more because their hourly wage is lower). But these losses, if they occur at all, might be a price worth paying for achieving a more justifiable overall distribution, and it might be offset by other, productivity-enhancing effects, stemming, for example, from the greater purchasing power in the hands of the average employee, which could fuel demand in the economy.

A third question concerns the *relations* of incomes in different jobs. For example, is it just, and justifiable among democratic citizens, that employees in care-related jobs earn less, on average, than employees in finance-related jobs? It may be very difficult to come up with standards of comparison for the different kinds of burden that comes with different jobs (and maybe also their different immaterial benefits, some of which may justify somewhat lower remuneration). Human beings are different, not only in terms of the values they pursue in life, but also in terms of talents and aptitudes. Therefore, different jobs are of different interest to them. Nonetheless, there are some burdens of jobs that create clear disadvantages, independent of specific personal preferences. For example, night shifts and irregular working hours have empirically proven negative effects on people's health (Pfeffer, 2018: chap. 2). Therefore, it is justified to require employers to pay higher remuneration for such work, both as a compensation to these employees and also as an incentive to keep such work to an absolute minimum.[13]

It might be objected that such measures for bringing labour markets more in line with democratic values are not feasible if undertaken only by some countries. In a globally competitive economy, it might be said, countries cannot afford to make labour more expensive, because this will lead to jobs being moved elsewhere. But while some international shifts in employment have certainly happened, it is noteworthy that despite global competition, one can still see 'varieties of capitalism', in the sense of different institutional settings in different countries (e.g. role and strength of unions, welfare state institutions, public service provision, etc.) (Hall and Soskice, 2001; Iversen and Soskice, 2019). How far countries could go in improving the conditions for labour, against the profit-motives of capital, is, ultimately, an empirical question.

But note that the conditions in the realm of capital are also not set in stone. Capital is constituted by legal relations (Pistor, 2013, 2019), and these relations,

---

[13] This is done in certain countries, e.g. Germany and Austria: shiftwork and work on weekends or public holidays receives higher remuneration than work in normal working hours.

like other property rights, can be changed. For example, it is no law of nature that capital flows need to be permitted to cross international borders unhindered, or that speculative investments can happen without (or with only minimal) taxation – instead of being discouraged, or slowed down, by a so-called 'Tobin tax' (Tobin, 1978). Moreover, there have recently been renewed discussions about the extent to which countries that have their own central bank can provide more money for public tasks, without risking dangerous levels of inflation ('modern monetary theory', see e.g. Kelton, 2020). Ultimately, the very nature of money is an open question: What is really 'given' about it, and what could be changed?

For reasons of space, I here cannot go into these discussions here (see e.g. Herzog, 2017; De Bruin et al., 2023; Sandberg and Warenski, 2024 for further discussions). The practical challenge is that fundamental reforms of the international financial and monetary system tend to happen only in or after major crises (e.g. the Bretton Woods arrangements after World War II). It is unclear how much change, especially at the international level, is politically feasible outside of such moments of rupture. But there is no reason to think that this area would not also, in principle, be open to reform. Instead of discussing financial and monetary reform in more detail, let me instead turn to an area in which reforms seem more feasible, and possible also outside of major global crises: the democratization of work.

3.2 Workplace Democracy[14]

Most individuals in modern societies work in organizations that are hierarchically organized: the internal logic of companies, but also of public administrations, is different from that of markets. It follows roughly the model of bureaucratic governance as described, for example, by Max Weber (1968 [1921], III: 956–8): there are different roles embedded in a hierarchical structure, in which those in higher positions give orders and coordinate the work of those in lower positions. As mentioned earlier, Coase (1937), in a famous paper, had explained why such hierarchies are often more efficient than markets: integrating workers into hierarchies lowers transaction costs. Instead of having to negotiate separately, for each task, what exactly workers would do and how much they would be paid, they enter a work contract, which contains an open-ended willingness to follow the orders of their bosses, in exchange for a salary.

Economists have continued this line of theorizing and suggested other reasons for why integration in hierarchies, instead of exchanges in markets, can be the more efficient solution. For example, integration in hierarchies can allow for firm-specific

---

[14] The following arguments follow, roughly, Herzog forthcoming.

investments in skills (Williamson, 1975). When workers collaborate in teams, it can be efficient to pay someone to supervise the whole team and prevent shirking (Alchian and Demsetz, 1972). Such arguments were often combined with an assumption that the owners of companies have the right to give orders to workers, even though, as economists and management scholars had also long noticed, in large companies, ownership (e.g. of shares by shareholders) and control (e.g. by managers) tend to be separated, leading to potential to conflicts of interests between them (Berle and Means, 1932). In any case, the right of those higher up in organizational hierarchies to hold power over the rest of the employees has not been much questioned in economic and management discourse. Many political philosophers and political scientists have also accepted it – maybe pointing to its limits (e.g. should employers be allowed to pressure employees into making political donations to causes they champion? See Hertel-Fernandez, 2018), but without questioning it at a fundamental level.

Against this widespread way of thinking, the idea of workplace democracy holds that the power of bosses in work organizations should be controlled by counterpower on the part of workers. Bosses have one-sided power over workers, and such power needs to be democratically legitimized (for the recent debate see in particular Anderson, 2017; Ferreras, 2017; Gould, 2019; for an overview see Frega et al., 2019). When first presented with this idea, individuals sometimes react with an intuitive rejection, thinking that the idea of 'democratic work' would mean the dissolution of all structures and a kind of spontaneous, anarchistic organization of work. They wonder how such forms of organizing work could be compatible with efficient outcomes. Another question is whether the 'democratization of work' would lead to the formation of informal power structures, for example, with the workers with the most essential functions forming powerful cliques and bossing others around.

To counter such worries, it is important to remember that 'democracy' as a principle of social order is not the same as anarchy, or as the complete absence of order. Democracy means, ultimately, rule by the people: those who live together under certain rules determined them together. For workplaces, the core constituency are the workers themselves, but scholars have debated to what extent other groups, for example, local residents or suppliers that strongly depend on a certain company, should also be involved in decision-making processes (e.g. Moriarty, 2010). Their joint rule-giving process can follow clear structures, and it can lead to some individuals or groups having power over others – but power that is democratically accountable, rather than one-sided and unchecked. Depending on one's theory of democracy, these structures can involve representative and participative formats (more on this below on p. 47). And just as in political democracy, they need to be combined with mechanisms that ensure the rule of law, for example to protect the rights of minorities. For workplace democracy, however, this 'rule of law' is ideally ensured by general laws (not just company-internal rules) which, for example, forbid discrimination against certain groups.

Let me first discuss workplace democracy as a principle at the level of ideal theory, without considering any feasibility constraints or questions of transition. Here, a famous argument that has been brought forward is the so-called parallel case argument: If one thinks that democracy is the right principle for governing the common affairs of people in the *political* realm, shouldn't one also think that it is the right principle for governing the common affairs of people in the *economic* realm? (e.g. Dahl, 1985). While this may appear a strong prima facie argument, it invites questions about the extent to which the parallel really holds, for example, whether the power bosses exercise over workers is as encompassing as that the government exercises over citizens (for discussions see, e.g., Landemore and Ferreras, 2016). To make progress in this discussion, it is helpful to ask what stands *behind* the imperative of democracy in the political realm, and whether these arguments also justify democracy in the economic realm, and specifically in the workplace.

A first argument for democracy builds on the equal moral standing of all members of society, which requires that they be given *equal voice* in political decisions (e.g. Christiano, 2008). This line of democratic theory has many commonalities with the liberal-egalitarian approach in political philosophy that I discussed earlier (in Section 1.2.1). The equal moral standing of all citizens is compatible with differences in positions that come about as a result of the democratic process; for example, the head of government of a representative democratic system has, in many ways, more voice than an ordinary citizen. But the powers and responsibilities of such roles are circumscribed by the rules of the democratic (and legal) system, they are democratically legitimized and limited in time. In principle, every citizen (above a certain age) is entitled to run for office. Those who hold an office are supposed to rule not for their private interest but for the public good – this, at least, are some of the principles of political democracy, though they are, sadly, often not realized in practice.

This argument can also be applied to workplaces: *functional* role differences, including differences in degrees of power that is democratically held to account, can be justified among moral equals, but they must not be organized such that the equal moral status of individuals is threatened. Critics of workplace democracy sometimes argue that workers accept employment contracts voluntarily and can exit them and work elsewhere if they are unhappy with the orders their boss gives them. But this argument is weaker than it may appear at first glance. Many workers do not have much of a choice when it comes to jobs, and even if they can shoulder the costs of moving to a different job, this often means that they simply have to work under *another* boss. And as long as most members of society have to work to provide for themselves and their families, the voluntariness of work is compromised (e.g. Anderson, 2017).

A second, related argument that can be understood as standing behind political democracy, and which is also transferrable to the context of work, concerns the distribution of power and counter-power. In a democracy, the real power is meant to lie with the people, and democratic institutions and practices (elections, campaigning, negotiations among members of parliament to organize majorities, etc.) are supposed to ensure this as much as possible. From this perspective – which can be linked to the neo-republican tradition – what matters is to effectively hold power to account. For the economic realm, it means asking about counterpower for *economic* power as well. This line of argument also leads to the role of unions, as organizations in which workers unite to resist the power of employers. Formal institutions, for example, co-determination in corporate boards, are insufficient, from that perspective, without the possibility of genuine threats on the side of employees, for example, through strikes (e.g. Gourevitch, 2018).

A third argument focusses on the capacities of citizens to lead truly democratic lives, both in the economic and in the political realm. This is not only a matter of seeing democracy as a 'way of life' that should permeate all spheres of social life, as Dewey (1939) had famously called it. It is also a question of giving citizens the opportunity to learn democratic habits and skills, and thereby to become competent democratic citizens (Pateman, 1970, chap. 3). This so-called 'spill-over argument' – that democratic competences and habits can be expected to 'spill over' from democratic workplaces to political engagement, and that political democracy can therefore be strengthened by democratizing work – has also been empirically explored, with mixed results (e.g. Carter, 2006; Schlachter and Ársaelsson, 2024). It is more plausible for forms of workplace democracy that involve not only *elected* worker representatives but also more *local* worker representation (e.g. through works councils) and opportunities to *participate directly* in deliberation and decision-making. No country has implemented full participatory workplace democracy, making empirical estimates difficult. However, data from Germany – a country with relatively far-ranging workers' rights – indicate that the existence of works councils and a cooperative, egalitarian culture at work (captured in the notion of 'industrial citizenship') are indeed correlated with stronger pro-democratic attitudes (Decker and Brähler, 2020; Pfeifer, 2023).

Thus, one might also argue for workplace democracy from the starting point that *political* democracy is currently not in great shape in many countries:

discontent is high, and many voters do not trust political institutions that are perceived as distant and elitist. Populist parties promise to speak for 'the people' and to provide easy solutions, often while playing racist and xenophobic cards (e.g. Mueller, 2017). The willingness to enter into reasonable dialogue with others seems to erode more and more, while negative emotions travel fast and wide on social media (Vosoughi et al., 2018). In this situation, some commentators suggest democratic innovations such as lottocratic citizen assemblies to renew democracy (Guerrero, 2014; Landemore, 2020). But these can, at best, reach a small number of people (Lafont, 2019). While democratizing workplaces may be a difficult task, it could, potentially, reach much larger numbers of people, and lead not only to shifts in how the economy functions but also to a strengthening of political democracy as a 'way of life'.[15]

Against these arguments in favour of workplace democracy, it might be objected that while these are attractive ideals, realizing them would come at the cost of other normatively important goods, such as the material welfare of all members of society or the opportunity for individuals to innovate and start new businesses. Sometimes, such arguments may be mere smokescreens meant to discredit proposals for more worker participation. But they can also come from a genuine concern for the welfare of societies or the economic freedom of their members. From that perspective, the question is: Is it possible to realize democratic principles at work without endangering other important values, which are realized through stable, efficient work organizations?

A first dimension of an answer to this question is to point to the fact that certain countries, especially in Scandinavia and Western Europe, have already implemented certain principles of democratic participation in workplaces, without companies having become dysfunctional (in fact, many of these companies successfully compete on global markets, in which many of their direct competitors are purely profit-oriented companies). For example, in many of these countries, corporate boards for large companies include seats for worker representatives, though hardly at the 50+ per cent that would be needed to grant true power to workers.[16] The effects of such co-determination have been controversially debated on theoretical grounds (e.g. Hansman, 1996). If one looks at empirical scholarship, it is clear that they are not negative – but also not overwhelmingly positive. There are some indications of slight improvements

---

[15] It is an open question in the discussion about workplace democracy what it could mean to democratize also forms of work that take place outside of regular jobs, e.g. unpaid housework or volunteering work.

[16] An exception is the German 'Montanmitbestimmung' (co-determination for mining and metal works) in which representatives of workers and shareholders have equal weight, with a neutral vote in case of a stalemate.

for workers, and higher degrees of substantive corporate responsibility measures that benefit third parties and the environment (e.g. Blandhol et al., 2020; Scholz and Vitols, 2019). For defenders of workplace democracy, this is good news in the sense that more democratically run companies are feasible and show some positive features. And yet, it does not say enough about what would happen to companies that would be truly democratically run.

Here, we can look at worker cooperatives, which provide another type of evidence about democratic workplaces. These do exist in many countries, and they are stable over time and do show many positive effects (e.g. Pérotin, 2016). But the number of cooperatives compared to the overall number of businesses is small, and many of them do not become very large (a famous exception is the group of Mondragon cooperatives in Spain, see e.g. Flecha and Santa Cruz 2011; Romeo 2022). So, the question arises as to what keeps the principle of worker cooperatives from being adopted on a wider scale. In the nineteenth century, John Stuart Mill had predicted that in the long run, all companies would become cooperatives, because individuals would no longer want to work for bosses who extract profits, and instead jointly run their own enterprises (2008 [1848/73]: 147).

This prediction has not become true, and so the question is whether this has to do with genuine functional deficits of democratic companies, or with factors in the current economic environment that favour non-democratic companies. The latter might have to do with path-dependencies and power relations that benefit non-democratic more than democratic companies. For example, one question that has been debated in the literature is whether worker cooperatives face obstacles concerning access to capital (Bowles and Gintis, 1994). If this is indeed a major problem, and if one otherwise considers worker cooperatives to be normatively superior to hierarchical workplaces, then programmes to support them could specifically target this issue. For example, a public investment bank could provide loans to cooperatives (Schweickart, 2011: chap. 3).

A second part of the answer to the feasibility objection is to admit that democratic organization may have some costs in terms of functionality – but that these costs are worth bearing, and that they might be outweighed by certain benefits, *also in terms of functionality*, of democratic workplaces. The latter argument, which emphasizes the *instrumental advantages* of democracy, runs as follows: yes, democratic decision-making is time-consuming and hence costly. But it can also have functional advantages, and it is a matter of designing good processes to harvest those. By picking the right tools from the toolbox of democratic practices and procedures, one can combine democracy and functionality. It is clear, for example, that in the emergency ward of a democratically run hospital, one would still need fast decision-making processes, to save the lives of patients. But this could happen by having either elected bosses, or rotating roles, together with an egalitarian culture in which all members of the team can make their voices heard and there is meaningful counterpower.

Indeed, one potential benefit of democratically organized work comes from the possibility of hearing different voices, and considering different perspectives, to come to the best possible solutions for the practical problems that need to be tackled by work teams. Take the medical context again: medical organizations have long known, and struggled with, the problem that the hierarchy between doctors and nursing staff leads to a lack of feedback and bad communication, with nurses not daring to speak up (e.g. Spencer et al., 2000). A more egalitarian culture, in which these different voices are all considered, might thus *improve*, rather than impair, the quality of decision-making. Such a culture is most likely to arise if there are indeed genuinely democratic structures, rather than if the power structures remain strictly hierarchical.

Parallel arguments hold in many other contexts: often, information flows from those doing the actual work and those making decisions about it are impaired, because the former fear the authority of the latter, and behave strategically – 'the boss only gets the good news' (Herzog, 2018: chap. VI). More democratic structures allow for the knowledge of more people to be put into the service of the intended outcomes.[17] Moreover, democratic decisions are likely to enjoy greater legitimacy among workers, so that the *implementation* of decisions is likely to be smoother than in the case of pure top-down decision-making, which might be met with resistance or even sabotage, for example, by 'work to rule' strategies.

Companies often try to reap these benefits by allowing for certain forms of participation, for example, through feedback formats or consultations. But their aim is typically only to increase the functionality of their operations, not to embody democratic values in their organization. Often, such attempts therefore remain limited to groups from which management hopes to gain information or who have high bargaining power, for example, highly skilled workers. Democratic work as a democratic ideal, in contrast, is meant to cover all workers; as such, it needs to be grounded in more than instrumental arguments. But the latter can play a supportive role in responding to objections to workplace democracy – similar to the role that instrumental arguments in favour of *political* democracy can play in responding to its critics.

Most existing workplaces today, however, are at quite some distance from realizing democratic principles, as ideal theory discusses them. What are possible non-ideal strategies that start in the here and now? To answer this

---

[17] This is an old argument that can already be found in Aristotle (*Politics* III, 11).

question, one needs to take into account the situation in different countries. In countries that already have a tradition of democratic work, it is a matter of strengthening and improving the institutions that give workers a voice: unions, works councils, or mechanisms for including worker representatives on corporate boards. Politically speaking, it seems wise to start from what is already there and to fight for improvements of these institutions and practices. The same holds for worker cooperatives: they are the purest form of workplace democracy, and political steps could be taken to strengthen them. In many European countries, there is an additional, pragmatic argument for doing this: because of demographic change, there will be a wave of retirements of company owners, especially of small and medium enterprises. The children of company owners are often not interested in taking over these businesses. Rather than liquidating companies or selling them off to competitors (and thus increasing market concentration, which is often undesirable for independent reasons), it can be an interesting option to facilitate the transition of ownership to employees (Gonza et al., 2021).

In countries in which no mechanisms of worker participation exist at this point, new models might also be tried. One such model is 'bicameralism', as suggested by Ferreras (2017; see also Ferreras et al., 2024). Taking inspiration from political moments in the history towards democracy in which power was shared with the masses, she suggests a system of two chambers of representatives, one selected by shareholders and one by workers, for large corporations. This, Ferreras argues, would amount to true power sharing. Arguably, however, the same goal could also be achieved by co-determination with genuine equality of votes (rather than a tie-breaking double-vote or a majority for shareholders, as is currently the case in most co-determination systems).

What matters for moving towards workplace democracy is perhaps less the concrete institutional form, but more the question of whether there is a genuine shift in power relations. This is a matter of formal structures, but it also has to do with wider social practices and the culture that prevails in companies, industries, and countries. For example, to what extent are crucial pieces of information shared proactively with all members of a co-determined board? Are decisions taken at the official meetings or through unofficial channels that favour one side over the other? It seems unlikely that genuine power-sharing will happen unless workers have a certain degree of bargaining power, for example, by being able to call a strike. The more antagonistic elements in labour relations may thus be not in contradiction to the more cooperative forms that one can often find in co-determined companies, but may rather be a precondition for the latter to function well. Worker representatives without power resources must be expected to be ineffective in protecting workers' interests, and may even be co-opted by the interests of shareholders.

This is also why the role of unions remains crucial for the project of increasing workers' voice at work and implementing democratic principles. Most workers are easily replaceable, from the perspective of employers, and as already noted, workers typically depend on their jobs as their main source of income. Hence, it is only as a collective that workers can increase their power. Historically, unions have also played an important role in building other capacities, for example, by creating educational opportunities for workers, supporting working-class artists, or publishing working-class newspapers. For example, the Workers' Educational Association, founded in the UK in 1903 and now also active in other countries, provides further education to thousands of working class people every year. In this way, unions also contributed to shaping different narratives that offered an alternative to the dominant economic accounts. This helped raise awareness and thereby, potentially, contributed to power along the third dimension that Lukes had distinguished (Lukes, 1974/2005, cf. above, p. 14–15).

Rebuilding union power, along these and other lines, will be a key task if the future of work is to be democratic. From the perspective of non-ideal theory, it is maybe the most important strategy that defenders of workplace democracy can, at this point, pursue. It can be endorsed from a liberal-egalitarian, neo-republican, and socialist perspective: the first can point to freedom of association and the need to protect workers' rights, the second to the need to counter employers' power, and the third to the building of capacity for more further-going changes in ownership structures. Political theorists can learn from theorists and practitioners of organizing about the strategies that can build worker power from the ground up (e.g. McAlevey, 2016; cf. also Bagg, 2024: chap. 10). As a way of redressing the massive imbalances of power in today's economic system, strengthening unions can also be a catalyst for other steps that make the economic system work better for all members of society, rather than benefit mostly a small elite.

3.3 Sustainable Work?

There is, however, yet another challenge for the future of work: how to make it compatible with planetary boundaries, that is, to make it ecologically sustainable? This imperative raises interesting questions from the perspective of political philosophy as well: What does it mean for work to be 'sustainable'? Can sustainability be understood exclusively in an environmental sense, or should it also be understood in a social sense? Who decides what counts as 'sustainable work'? What does it mean for the power relations between workers and employers to make work 'sustainable'? And can this happen within a capitalist system, or does it require stepping out of the growth logic of capitalism, towards a 'post-growth' scenario? (e.g. Cassiers et al., 2018). Can 'sustainable work' be achieved with a few tweaks here and there, for example higher taxes on CO_2 emissions, or does it require a more fundamental rethinking of the *point* of our economic activities and our relations to nature?

These questions have, arguably, not been sufficiently addressed by political philosophers. In all three traditions I have distinguished – liberal-egalitarian, neo-republican, and Marxist/critical theory – there exist discussions about climate change and the environment (e.g. Kim, 2019; Töns, 2023 from a liberal-egalitarian perspective; e.g. Barry, 2008 from a neo-republican perspective; e.g. Foster, 2023 from an eco-Marxist perspective). But these have not yet been sufficiently integrated into discussions about the future of work, and of economic philosophy in general. The most far-ranging discussions can be found in eco-Marxist thinking, which is not surprising: it provides the most critical perspective on the current economic system and can thus also easily integrate criticisms from an ecological perspective. And yet, a key problem remains what to do with these damning diagnoses of the current system: What better system is possible, and how can one get there?

While 'green jobs' is a slogan used in the international policy literature, taking the call for 'sustainable work' seriously is far more demanding (see for the following Herzog and Zimmermann 2025). Work should not only be sustainable in an environmental sense but also be 'socially sustainable' in the sense that it does not exhaust or harm individual workers and their social relations. Unpaid forms of work, for example, care work done in families, should be part of the picture, too, as should be local and global interrelations, for example in supply to chains, to make sure that unsustainable forms of work are not simply outsourced to other, typically poorer, countries. The question is also what the normative bases for claims to sustainability, and hence sustainable work, are: Is work understood as satisfying preferences (as in standard economic theories), needs, or capabilities? But what, then, if conflicts arise between the different dimensions of sustainability?

Some critics of the current work regime argue that today's unsustainable forms of work – along many of these dimensions – have to do with a consumerist lifestyle in which individuals work far longer than they would like to, to 'keep up with the Jones' (e.g. Schor, 1992, 1998; for a philosophical discussion see also Thomas et al. 2025, chap. 9). Some have therefore called for a reduction of work time, for example, through a four-day work week, which has recently been tried out in a large-scale UK experiment, with overall positive results for workers (Autonomy, 2023). It might be tempting to think that the reduction of work time could also increase environmental sustainability, for example, through reduced energy consumption (e.g. Hickel, 2020: 221–222). But whether or not this happens is likely to depend on many contextual factors in the wider economic system (e.g. Pullinger, 2014).

The debate about a sustainable future of the economy has, to a great extent, taken place within environmental and other heterodox schools of economics. Here, the 'postgrowth' discussion has been particularly intense: Should societies step away from the political goal of economic growth, in order to protect the environment (e.g. Hickel, 2020; Jackson, 2021)? Or is it exactly through economic growth, but of the 'green' kind (e.g. Terzi, 2022), that the transition towards a sustainable economic system can be achieved? This debate is very fierce, and yet there is also a lot of common ground between the different camps (Herzog, 2025: chap. 4). All sides agree that a reduction of resource use and emissions is necessary in the developed economies,[18] and that economic growth of the kind capitalist countries have seen in the past is incompatible with such a reduction. Thus, the question becomes either, for the 'green growth' camp, how to shift the economic systems away from traditional, towards 'green' growth, or, for the 'postgrowth' camp, how growth, at least of the harmful kind, can be stopped.

Both questions lead back to questions about power, and about the relation between politics and the economy: *Can* democratic politics impose rules on the economy that move it in a green direction? Or will all such attempts lead to mere 'green washing' and pseudo-solutions, because economic players are so powerful that they can thwart all attempts to introduce real change? It has already become public knowledge that the fossil fuel and other traditional industries use various manoeuvres to spread climate change denialism and to influence politics in their own favour (Cook et al., 2019). These industries had learned from the experiences of other industries, notably tobacco, earlier on, on how to delay regulation that serves the general interest but constitutes a threat to their own business model. The so-called 'tobacco strategy' includes measures such as providing support for researchers who explore alternative explanations of the harmful phenomenon, sowing doubt about scientific research, and obfuscating the public and political discourse (Oreskes and Conway, 2010).

To connect this point back to the question of 'sustainable work': clearly, many companies have an interest in presenting their business models, and hence

---

[18] In poor countries, economic growth is still needed to satisfy the basic needs of all members of society, and it is unlikely that this can happen without *any* increases in emissions. From a perspective of global justice, one can argue that this reinforces the normative pressure on richer countries to cut their emissions even *more* quickly, to create more space for other countries to grow.

also the jobs that are part of it, as 'green'. For example, the mining of rare earths metals – which often has destructive environmental and social impacts in the regions in which it happens – can be presented as 'sustainable work' if these materials are used for batteries for electric cars (Zbyszewska and Maximo, 2025). To prevent such one-sided claims, one obviously needs a broader concept of sustainable work that takes its various dimensions into account. But to evaluate these dimensions, to understand how they relate to each other, and to see which trade-offs might be necessary, it is crucial to hear the voices of those who are actually concerned with the work in question and its effects. Thus, questions about sustainable work lead back to questions about who has a say about work: Can workers bring in their perspectives? Who has the power to define the metrics that are used to measure progress towards 'green work'? (Herzog and Zimmerman, 2025). What role can unions play in a 'just transition' towards a sustainable economy (Stevis and Felli, 2015)? Such questions will likely shape labour relations in the years to come.

Ultimately, it is clear that both for the sake of democracy *and* for the sake of sustainability, it is not enough to consider work in abstraction from other features of the economic system. The question is not just what kind of *work* democratic societies want but also what kind of *markets* they want, what kind of *public provision* they want and, ultimately, what the *point and purpose* of the economic system is. Economists had long seen the latter as a private question: individuals, as private consumers, should decide, via their purchasing decisions, what the economic system produces. This seemed an elegant way of avoiding value conflicts and of presenting economic policies as value-neutral and non-paternalistic (Ciepley, 2007). But this position is no longer tenable in the face of the climate crisis. Moreover, with ever-increasing inequality, the argument that individuals can vote with their wallets, in the market, becomes a cynical smokescreen: only those with sufficient purchasing power for, for example, organic food or electric cars, can influence the economic system in this way.

It is time to have a broader public debate about what it is that we want from the economy. The current model has become too dysfunctional to be seen as legitimate. Even if one may end up re-endorsing *some* of its elements, this needs to happen against the background of a more fundamental questioning of what the economy is supposed to do, and how democratic politics can stir it in this direction – whether in the traditional way, by setting the rules from the outside, or through a thorough-going internal democratization, as I have defended it here.

In the concluding section, I summarize my arguments and reflect on what this means, in the current moment, for the research strategies that political philosophers can use to understand possible alternatives.

4 Conclusion

In this *Element* I have discussed the relation between politics and the economy from three philosophical traditions. The liberal egalitarian tradition emphasizes in particular the equal moral worth of all individuals and asks what institutions and practices can embody this principle. This perspective can, for example, be used for a criticism of market practices in which individuals do not show mutual respect but exploit the vulnerabilities of others. The neo-republican tradition focuses in particular on the critique of one-sided, arbitrary power. This makes it very suitable for analysing power relations in markets, especially labour markets. The socialist tradition, which often overlaps with critical theory, asks fundamental questions about the dynamics of capitalist competition and the need to overcome it. As such, its attention to the distribution of property rights and the power that flows from it is of particular interest for understanding the economy.

In other periods, the philosophical discourse about the economy might concentrate on figuring out the relations between these different traditions. One might want to explore which principles and values, but also which assumptions about the ontology of the economic realm and about human nature, stand behind them. This remains an important task also today. And yet, as I have tried to show, when it comes to criticizing today's economic system, there is also a lot of overlap. Even though the criticisms come from different directions, and theorists from different camps have different long-term visions of what an alternative economic system should look like, they could, arguably, do more to join forces.

I have demonstrated this point with regard to several topics. When it comes to the relation between economic and political power, all three traditions agree that there is currently a need to 'tame' markets: to keep them out of certain social spheres and to limit their overall influence on society. There is disagreement on whether the only, or most promising, strategy to achieve this is through changes in property rights in the means of production, or whether other strategies are also possible. I have argued that the latter seems plausible, given the many different forms that power can take, beyond property rights. But the chances of success will, in my views, remain limited if one sticks to a traditional model of the 'primacy of politics', that is democratic politics setting the rules of the economic system, rather than embedding democratic principles in the economy in a deeper way.

I have then zoomed in to the organization of work as an area in which such an 'embedding' of democratic principles should take place. I have discussed the justice of wages as a matter of the democratic commitment to moral equality and the complementarity of different jobs. Moreover, in a democracy, democratic values should also be embedded in workplaces. From all three philosophical traditions, there is an urgent imperative, in today's situation, to strengthen workers' voice, by rebuilding unions or finding other ways of organizing workers. Last but not least, there are also questions about how democracies can make work – and their economic systems more broadly speaking – sustainable in an environmental sense, broadly understood. Can this happen in economic systems that remain committed to economic growth, or does it require a post-growth scenario? These questions lead back to questions about power: how can democratic societies shape their economic systems in ways that bring them in line with planetary boundaries?

All in all, my arguments amount to a plea for a more integrated way of thinking about politics and the economy. More specifically, I have argued that the separation into a democratic political system and an economic system that follows a completely different logic is unlikely to be stable in the long run. In fact, in most historical societies, the logics of the political and economic system were more in line; what is unusual, from a historical perspective, is precisely the *separation* of these logics (see also Meiksins Wood, 1995: chap. 1). Democratic societies have a stark choice to make: either to bring their economic systems more in line with democratic values – or risk losing their democratic systems in the political realm, which threaten to be undermined by the highly unequal power dynamics that already dominate the economic realm (see also Fleurbaey, 2006; Herzog, 2025).[19]

There is some historical evidence that backs up this worry. The economic historian van Bavel (2016) has explored various historical cases of market economies, in which factor markets (markets in land, labour, and capital) arose, for example, in ancient Persia and the early modern Netherlands. Initially, this led to an increase in general welfare, but over time, economic elites captured political power and changed the rules of the economic game in their own favour, closing down the welfare-enhancing dynamics. Van Bavel presents this as a general pattern, in a way that may be criticized for sounding all too deterministic. But there is a real question about today's situation, and the power of democratic society to resist these inegalitarian tendencies.

---

[19] Of course, I am not claiming that this is the *only* threat to political democracy. The current form of right-wing populism that despises the rule of law and a rule-bound approach to democratic conflict is shot through with racist, xenophobic, and anti-feminist dimensions. The direct fight against these latter trends is, of course, also crucial. But I take it that improving the economic situation of the population, reducing the degree of economic insecurity and rebuilding 'good jobs' is an important *indirect* strategy against these trends as well, because insecurity or a feeling of being left behind, or being disadvantaged compared to other groups, is one of their underlying causes (cf. e.g. Hochschild 2016, on the feeling of Trump voters of being left behind and disadvantaged compared to women and members of minorities).

What are the chances of moving towards a more just and more sustainable economic system? It is easy to despair about this question – but this is unlikely to be the right moral answer, especially for those individuals who belong to the more privileged strata of Western societies. In a comparative global perspective, they still have many personal freedoms and opportunities for agency. They can find manifold ways of making a difference, in large and small ways – as voters, as consumers, or as members of civil society associations (see also Schweickart, 2011: chap. 6).

What about political philosophers – what role can their work play in this situation? While there is a difference between research and activism, all researchers need to make decisions about their research topics, and these inevitably involve value judgements. There are at least three areas in which contributions by political philosophers can play an important role for moving towards a different relation between politics and the economy.

The first is the critique of narratives and assumptions about the lack of alternatives – the famous 'TINA' ('there is no alternative') claim that UK prime minister Margaret Thatcher started, and that has been repeated all too often. In political discourse, many ideas that have long been proven wrong by academic research live on – in a form of 'zombie economics', as Quiggin (2010) has called it. Political philosophers, but also researchers from legal studies, sociology, the history of ideas and many other fields, do important work in explaining what is wrong with such ideas, how they historically arose and seemed plausible at the time, and why they do not help to understand today's situation. In critical theory, 'ideology critique' contributes to this endeavour, but it is also practiced by many other scholars, in somewhat different methodological approaches, with the shared aim of showing the historical contingency (or plain wrongness) of what is all too often taken for granted. For example, the idea that states should limit their debts and aim for a balanced budget, if necessary by cutting welfare expenses ('austerity'), has been subjected to detailed scrutiny (e.g. Blyth, 2015).

A second strategy is to bring the voices of those individuals who experience current economic practices and institutions from the disadvantaged side into academic and public discourse. Of course, in an ideal world, researchers would come from all kinds of class and ethnic backgrounds and have social networks in different parts of society. As a matter of fact, academia, in many countries, is overwhelmingly white and from privileged backgrounds. This makes it all the more important to not only rely on one's own moral intuitions and assumptions about what is or is not important about the current economic system, but listen also to other voices. Such approaches have, in recent years, come under different labels, for example, 'ethnographic sensibility' (Herzog and Zacka, 2019; Longo and Zacka, 2019) or 'grounded theory' (Ackerly et al., 2024). The latter has stronger connections with older approaches in social science research such as 'action research' (e.g. de Koning and Martin, 1996), and one can also draw a line to the notion of 'citizen science', which is more widely used in the natural sciences, but can also be applied to the social sciences (Hecker et al., 2018; Herzog and Lepenies, 2022).

A third research approach is to explore alternatives to the current economic system, in collaboration with those practitioners who experiment with new economic practices and institutions. Erik Olin Wright (2010) has dubbed such cases 'real utopias'. Exploring them helps understand what makes some of these cases a success (and others a failure – the analysis of failures is a strategy that could probably be used more, to understand how economic institutions and practices work). This is important for thinking through the possibility of mainstreaming them, both in substance and also for political reasons: with concrete examples at hand, one can make a more convincing case in public discourse that one is not just indulging in unrealistic fantasies. A recent example are the large-scale experiments with a four-day work week mentioned in section 3.3, which were conducted by an alliance of researchers, think tanks, and companies (e.g. Autonomy, 2023). They brought not only interesting insights but also led to increased interest in the topic in the media and public discourse.

A danger with this latter approach, however, is that it might create the impression that there is need for experimentation on *all* fronts before any concrete reform steps could ever be taken. This is far from the truth. There are many institutional solutions that have been tried and tested in one or several countries and that could be adopted elsewhere, for example, in the fight against labour exploitation. There are also insights from history, for example, that corporate taxes had been far higher in the past without causing the kinds of inefficiencies and distortions that corporations warn against whenever tax increases are being discussed today. There are many steps that governments could, with sufficient confidence, take already now. The energy for large-scale experimenting should go only into those areas where there is a genuine need for new knowledge.

The second and third strategies I have suggested imply that researchers should, to some extent, break down the walls that all too often separate academia from practice, and find ways of undertaking research together with societal actors. The point is not to erase the difference between experts and lay people but to bring *different* forms of knowledge and experience together, to uncover own blind spots and to find more integrated ways of understanding the phenomena in question. Such collaborative practices have been tried and tested in different fields, and they can offer a potential for improving democratic governance, both in the sense of coming to better solutions but also in the sense of better integrating citizens' voices (e.g. Dzur, 2018).

There is an irony here, however. Such collaborative research projects take time to build trust between different parties, they may not deliver immediate results, or they may deliver results that do not 'count' in the currencies of academic merit measurement. In many countries, academia has itself been subjected to a logic of efficiency that goes hand in hand with quantitative measurement of 'output', the deliberate creation of a competitive culture, and the precarization of academic employment (see, e.g., Bone, 2021). This makes it more difficult for many researchers to engage in the kinds of long-term, collaborative projects that could best contribute to the search for alternatives to the current economic system.

Nonetheless, there are still many opportunities for academics to engage in such projects; I have sketched three strategies but there are also many others. By choosing such strategies, researchers can consciously adopt a democratic agenda, all while staying committed to highest epistemic standards of rigorous scholarship and research. This may go against the logic of (self-)marketization in academia, and may not be feasible for everyone. And yet, it is a role of academia – with the public trust that it still enjoys – that democratic societies could massively benefit from. In that sense, for political philosophers, the choice for the values of democracy, to resist the expanding logic of markets, begins very much at home.

References

Acemoglou, D., and Robinson, J. 2012. *Why Nations Fail: The Origins of Power, Prosperity, and Poverty*. New York: Crown Business.

Ackerly, B., Cabrera, L., Forman, G. et al. 2024. 'Unearthing Grounded Normative Theory: Practices and Commitments of Empirical Research in Political Theory'. *Critical Review of International Social and Political Philosophy* 27(2), 156–182.

Adler, P. S. 2019. *The 99 Percent Economy: How Democratic Socialism Can Overcome the Crises of Capitalism*. New York: Oxford University Press.

Agmon, S. 2021. 'Undercutting Justice: Why Legal Representation Should Not Be Allocated by the Market'. *Politics, Philosophy & Economics* 20(1), 99–123.

Al Salman, Y. 2022. 'Independence in the Commons: How Group Ownership Realises Basic Non-Domination'. In M. Bennett, H. Brouwer, and R. Claassen (eds.), *Wealth and Power: Philosophical Perspectives*. New York: Routledge, 206–225.

Alchian, A. A., and Demsetz, H. 1972. 'Production, Information Costs, and Economic Organization.' *American Economic Review* 62, 777–795.

Alesina, A., Glaeser, E., and Sacerdote, B. 2005. 'Work and Leisure in the United States and Europe: Why So Different?' *NBER Macroeonomics Annual* 20, 1–64.

Allen, A. 1999. *The Power of Feminist Theory: Domination, Resistance, Solidarity*. Boulder: Westview Press.

Anderson, E. 1999. 'What Is the Point of Equality?' *Ethics* 109(2), 287–337.

Anderson, E. 2013. *The Imperative of Integration*. Princeton: Princeton University Press.

Anderson, E. 2017. *Private Government: How Employers Rule Our Lives (and Why We Don't Talk about It)*. Princeton: Princeton University Press.

Apostolidis, P. 2018. *The Fight for Time: Migrant Day Laborers and the Politics of Precarity*. Oxford: Oxford University Press.

Aristotle. 1984. 'Politics'. In J. Barnes (ed.), *The Complete Works of Aristotle*, vol. II. Princeton: Princeton University Press, 1986–2129.

Atkinson, A. B. 2015. *Inequality: What Can Be Done?* Cambridge, MA: Harvard University Press.

Autonomy. 2023. *The Results Are In: The UK's Four-Day Week Pilot*. Hampshire: Autonomy Research Ltd.

Bachrach, P., and Baratz, M. S. 1962. 'The Two Faces of Power'. *American Political Science Review* 56(4), 941–952.

Bagg, S. E. 2024. *The Dispersion of Power: A Critical Realist Theory of Democracy*. New York: Oxford University Press.

Baradaran, M. 2015. *How the Other Half Banks*: Exclusion, Exploitation, and the Threat to Democracy. Cambridge, MA: Harvard University Press.

Barca, S. 2020. *Forces of Reproduction*: Notes for a Counter-Hegemonic Anthropocene. Cambridge: Cambridge University Press.

Bardhan, P., and Roemer, J. E. (eds.). 1993. *Market Socialism: The Current Debate*. New York: Oxford University Press.

Barry, J. 2008. 'Towards a Green Republicanism: Constitutionalism, Political Economy, and the Green State'. *The Good Society* 17(2), 4–11.

Beck, V. 2018. 'Consumer Boycotts as Instruments for Structural Change'. *Journal of Applied Philosophy* 36(4), 543–559.

Bennett, M. 2021. 'The Capital Flight Quadrilemma: Democratic Trade-Offs and International Investment'. *Ethics & Global Politics* 14(4), 199–217.

Berkey, B. 2021. 'Ethical Consumerism, Democratic Values, and Justice'. *Philosophy & Public Affairs* 49, 237–274.

Berle, A., and Means, G. 1932. *The Modern Corporation and Private Property*. Piscataway: Transaction.

Berman, S. 2006. *The Primacy of Politics*: Social Democracy and the Making of Europe's Twentieth Century. Cambridge: Cambridge University Press.

Bertrand, E., and Panitch, V. (eds.). 2024. *The Routledge Handbook of Commodification*. London: Routledge.

Blandhol, C., Mogstad, M., Nilsson, P., and Vestad, O. L. 2020. 'Do Employees Benefit from Worker Representation on Corporate Boards?' *NBER Working Paper* No. 28269.

Block, S., and Sachs, S. 2020. 'Clean Slate for Worker Power: Building a Just Economy and Democracy', January 2020. Labor and Worklife Program at Harvard Law School, (https://lwp.law.harvard.edu/files/lwp/files/full_report_clean_slate_for_worker_power.pdf).

Blyth, M. 2015. *Austerity*: The History of a Dangerous Idea. New York: Oxford University Press.

Bone, K. D. 2021. 'Cruel Optimism and Precarious Employment: The Crisis Ordinariness of Academic Work'. *Journal of Business Ethics* 174, 275–290.

Bowles, S., and Gintis, H. 1994. 'Credit Market Imperfections and the Incidence of Worker-Owned Firms'. *Metroeconomica* 45(3), 209–223.

Bradford, A. 2020. *The Brussels Effect: How the European Union Rules the World*. Oxford: Oxford University Press.

Brennan, J., and Jaworski, P. M. 2015. 'Markets without Symbolic Limits'. *Ethics* 125(4), 1053–1077.

Bruni, L., and Sugden, R. 2008. 'Fraternity: Why the Market Need Not Be a Morally Free Zone'. *Economics and Philosophy* 24, 35–64.

Burgin, A. 2012. *The Great Persuasion: Reinventing Free Markets since the Depression*. Cambridge, MA: Harvard University Press.

Cagé, J. 2020. *The Price of Democracy: How Money Shapes Politics and What to Do about It*. Cambridge, MA: Harvard University Press.

Carens, J. H. 1981. *Equality, Moral Incentives, and the Market: An Essay in Utopian Politico-Economic Theory*. Chicago: The University of Chicago Press.

Carter, N. 2006. 'Political Participation and the Workplace: The Spillover Thesis Revisited'. *British Journal of Politics and International Relations* 8(3), 410–426.

Cassiers, I., Marechal, K., and Méda, D. (eds.). 2018. *Post-Growth Economics and Society: Exploring the Paths of a Social and Ecological Transition*. London: Routledge.

Chetty, R. 2018. 'Raj Chetty on "The Lost Einsteins"'. 11 January. www.brookings.edu/events/raj-chetty-on-the-lost-einsteins/.

Christiano, T. 2008. *The Constitution of Equality: Democratic Authority and Its Limits*. Oxford: Oxford University Press.

Christiano, T. 2012. 'Money in Politics'. In D. Estlund (ed.), *The Oxford Handbook of Political Philosophy*. Oxford: Oxford University Press, 241–258.

Christophers, B. 2023. *Our Lives in Their Portfolios: Why Asset Managers Own the World*. London: Verso.

Ciepley, D. 2007. *Liberalism in the Shadow of Totalitarianism*. Cambridge, MA: Harvard University Press.

Ciepley, D. 2013. 'Beyond Public and Private: Toward a Political Theory of the Corporation'. *American Political Science Review* 107(1), 139–158.

Claassen, R., and Herzog, L. 2019. 'Why Economic Agency Matters: An Account of Structural Domination in the Economic Realm'. *European Journal of Political Theory*, online first March 9.

Claassen, R., and Herzog, L. 2021. 'Making Power Explicit: Why Liberal Egalitarians Should Take (Economic) Power Seriously'. *Social Theory and Practice*, online first, 14 April, www.pdcnet.org/soctheorpract/content/soctheorpract_2021_0999_4_7_119.

Coase, R. H. 1937. 'The Nature of the Firm'. *Economica*, New Series 4(16), 386–405.

Cohen, G. A. 1989. 'On the Currency of Egalitarian Justice'. *Ethics* 99, 906–944.

Cohen, G. A. 1991. 'Incentives, Inequality, and Community'. *The Tanner Lectures on Human Values*, Stanford: May 21, 23.

Cohen, G. A. 1997. 'Where the Action Is: On the Site of Distributive Justice'. *Philosophy & Public Affairs* 26(1), 3–30.

Conway, E. M., and Oreskes, N. 2023. *The Big Myth: How American Business Taught Us to Loathe Government and Love the Free Market*. London: Bloomsbury.

Cook, J., Supran, G., Lewandowsky, S., Oreskes, N., and Maibach, E. 2019. *America Misled: How the Fossil Fuel Industry Deliberately Misled Americans about Climate Change*. Fairfax: George Mason University Center for Climate Change Communication.

Cornell, A. B., and Barenberg, M. (eds.). 2022. *The Cambridge Handbook of Labor and Democracy*. Cambridge: Cambridge University Press.

Crenshaw, K. 1989. 'Demarginalizing the Intersection of Race and Sex: A Black Feminist Critique of Anti-discrimination Doctrine Feminist Theory and Antiracist Politics'. *University of Chicago Legal Forum* 1(8), 139–167.

Cumbers, A. 2020. *The Case for Economic Democracy*. Cambridge: Polity.

Cunningham, F. 2005. 'Market Economies and Market Societies'. *Journal of Social Philosophy* 36(2), 129–142.

Dahl, R. 1985. *A Preface to Economic Democracy*. Berkeley: University of California Press.

Danaher, J. 2019. *Automation and Utopia: Human Flourishing in an Age without Work*. Cambridge, MA: Harvard University Press.

de Bruin, B., Herzog, L., O'Neill, M., and Sandberg, J. 2023. 'Philosophy of Money and Finance'. *The Stanford Encyclopedia of Philosophy* (Spring 2023 Edition), Edward N. Zalta & Uri Nodelman (eds.), <https://plato.stanford.edu/archives/spr2023/entries/money-finance/>.

De Koning, K., and Martin, M. (eds.). 1996. *Participatory Research in Health: Issues and Experiences*. London: Zed Books.

De Stefano, V. 2019. '"Negotiating the Algorithm": Automation, Artificial Intelligence and Labour Protection'. *Comparative Labor Law & Policy Journal* 41(1), 1–32.

Decker, O., and Brähler, E. (eds.). 2020. *Autoritäre Dynamiken: Alte Ressentiments – neue Radikalität*. Gießen: Psychosozial-Verlag.

Dewey, J. 1939. 'Creative Democracy: The Task before Us'. In *John Dewey and the Promise of America*. Columbus: American Education Press, 12–17.

Dietsch, P. 2010. 'The Market, Competition and Equality'. *Politics, Philosophy & Economics* 9(2), 213–244.

Dietsch, P. 2015. *Catching Capital – The Ethics of Tax Competition*. New York: Oxford University Press.

Dietsch, P., Claveau, F., and Fontan, C. 2018. *Do Central Banks Serve the People?* Cambridge: Polity Press.

Doppelt, G. 1981. 'Rawls' System of Justice: A Critique from the Left'. *Noûs* 15(3), 259–307.

Dowding, K. (ed.). 2011. *Encyclopedia of Power*. Los Angeles: Sage.

Dworkin, R. 1981a. 'What Is Equality? Part 1: Equality of Welfare'. *Philosophy and Public Affairs* 10(3), 185–246.

Dworkin, R. 1981b. 'What Is Equality? Part 2: Equality of Resources'. *Philosophy and Public Affairs* 10(4), 283–345.

Dworkin, R. 2000. *Sovereign Virtue: The Theory and Practice of Equality*. Cambridge, MA: Harvard University Press.

Dzur, A. 2018. *Democracy Inside: Participatory Innovation in Unlikely Places*. New York: Oxford University Press.

Edmundson, J. 2017. *Rawls: Reticent Socialist*. Cambridge: Cambridge University Press.

Engels, F. 1845/1969. *The Conditions of the Working Class in England*. Marxist.org archive.

Federici, S. 2012. *Revolution at Point Zero: Housework, Reproduction, and Feminist Struggle*. Oakland: PM Press.

Ferreras, I. 2017. *Firms as Political Entities: Saving Democracy through Economic Bicameralism*. Cambridge: Cambridge University Press.

Ferreras, I., Malleson, T., Rogers, J. (eds.). 2024. *Democratizing the Corporation: The Bicameral Firm and Beyond*. London: Verso.

Flecha, R., and Santa Cruz, I. 2011. 'Cooperation for Economic Success: The Mondragon Case'. *Anaylse & Kritik* 33(1), 157–170.

Fleurbaey, M. 2006. *Capitalisme ou démocratie? L'alternative du XXIème siècle*. Paris: Grasset.

Foster, J. B. 2023. 'Planned Degrowth: Ecosocialism and Sustainable Human Development'. *Monthly Review* 75(3).

Frankfurt, H. 1987. 'Equality as a Moral Ideal'. *Ethics* 98(1), 21–43.

Fraser, N. 2013. 'How Feminism Became Capitalism's Handmaiden – and How to Reclaim It'. *The Guardian*, 14 October.

Fraser, N. 2023. *Cannibal Capitalism: How our System Is Devouring Democracy, Care, and the Planet – and What We Can Do about It*. London: Verso.

Freeman, S. 2011. 'Capitalism in the Classical and High Liberal Traditions'. *Social Philosophy and Policy* 28, 19–55.

Frega, R., Herzog, L., and Neuhäuser, C. 2019. 'Workplace Democracy – the Recent Debate'. *Philosophy Compass* 14(4), e12574.

Fricker, M. 2007. *Epistemic Injustice: Power and the Ethics of Knowing*. New York: Oxford University Press.

Friedman, S., and Laurison, D. 2019. *The Class Ceiling: Why It Pays to Be Privileged*. Bristol: Bristol University Press.

Gädeke, D. 2020. 'Does a Mugger Dominate? Episodic Power and the Structural Dimension of Domination'. *Journal of Political Philosophy* 28(2), 199–221.

Gaus, G. 2012. 'Property'. In D. Estlund (ed.), *The Oxford Handbook of Political Philosophy*. Oxford: Oxford University Press, 93–112.

Gilabert, P., and O'Neill, M. 2024. 'Socialism'. *The Stanford Encyclopedia of Philosophy*, Edward N. Zalta & Uri Nodelman (eds.), forthcoming https://plato.stanford.edu/archives/sum2024/entries/socialism/.

Gonza, T., Ellerman, D., Berkopec, G., Žgank, T., and Široka, T. 2021. 'Marcora for Europe: How Worker-Buyouts Might Help Save Jobs and Build Resilient Businesses'. *European State Aid Law Quarterly* 20(1), 61–73.

Gould, C. C. 2019. 'Protecting Democracy by Extending It: Democratic Management Reconsidered'. *Journal of Social Philosophy* 50(4), 513–535.

Gourevitch, A. 2018. 'The Right to Strike: A Radical View'. *American Political Science Review* 112(4), 905–912.

Grey, T. C. 1980. 'The Disintegration of Property'. In J. R. Pennock and J. W. Chapman (eds.), *NOMOS XXII: Property*. New York: New York University Press, 69–85.

Guerrero, A. 2014. 'Against Elections: The Lottocratic Alternative'. *Philosophy and Public Affairs* 42(2), 135–178.

Hacker, J. 2011. *The Institutional Foundations of Middle-Class Democracy*, Policy Network, 6 May.

Hall, P. A., and Soskice, D. 2001. 'An Introduction to Varieties of Capitalism'. In P. A. Hall and D. Soskice (eds.), *Varieties of Capitalism: The Institutional Foundations of Comparative Advantage*. Oxford: Oxford University Press, 1–68.

Hansman, H. 1996. *The Ownership of Enterprise*. Cambridge, MA: Harvard University Press.

Hardin, G. 1986. 'The Tragedy of the Commons'. *Science* 162(3859), 1243–1248.

Harsanyi, J. C. 1975. 'Review: Can the Maximin Principle Serve as a Basis for Morality? A Critique of John Rawls'. *American Political Science Review* 69(2), 594–606.

Hausman, D. 2021. 'Philosophy of Economics'. In Edward N. Zalta (ed.), *The Stanford Encyclopedia of Philosophy*, <https://plato.stanford.edu/archives/win2021/entries/economics/>.

Hayek, F. A. 1944. *The Road to Serfdom*. London: Routledge.

Hayek, F. A. 1945. 'The Use of Knowledge in Society'. *American Economic Review* 35(4), 519–530.

Heath, J. 2014. *Morality, Competition, and the Firm: The Market Failures Approach to Business Ethics*. New York: Oxford University Press.

Heath, J., Moriarty, J., and Norman, W. 2010. 'Business Ethics and (or as) Political Philosophy'. *Business Ethics Quarterly* 20(3), 427–452.

Hecker, S., Haklay, M., Bowser, A., et al. (eds.) 2018. *Citizen Science: Innovation in Open Science, Society and Policy*. London: UCL Press.

Heldt, E., and Herzog, L. 2022. 'The Limits of Transparency: Expert Knowledge and Meaningful Accountability in Central Banking'. *Government & Opposition* 57(2), 217–232.

Hertel Ferandez, A. 2018. *Politics at Work: How Companies Turn Their Workers into Lobbyists*. New York: Oxford University Press.

Herzog, L. (ed.). 2017. *Just Financial Markets? Finance in a Just Society*. Oxford: Oxford University Press.

Herzog, L. 2018. *Reclaiming the System: Moral Responsibility, Divided Labour, and the Role of Organizations in Society*. Oxford: Oxford University Press.

Herzog, L. 2021. 'Global Reserve Currencies from the Perspective of Structural Global Justice: Distribution and Domination'. *Critical Review of International Social and Political Philosophy* 24(7), 931–953.

Herzog, L. 2022. 'Equal Dignity For All Citizens Mean Equal Voice at Work: The Importance of Epistemic Justice'. In I. Ferreras, J. Battilana, and D. Méda (eds.), *Democratize Work: The Case for Reorganizing the Economy*. Chicago: The University of Chicago Press, 55–60.

Herzog, L. 2023. *Citizen Knowledge: Markets, Experts, and the Infrastructure of Democracy*. New York: Oxford University Press.

Herzog, L. 2024a. 'Bodies at Work: The Normative Dimensions of the Geography of Work'. *Social Theory and Practice* 50(1), 57–79.

Herzog, L. 2024b. 'Liberal Egalitarianism beyond Methodological Atomism'. In I. Robeyns (eds.), *Pluralizing Political Philosophy: Economic and Ecological Inequalities in Global Perspective*. Oxford: Oxford University Press, 107–130.

Herzog, L. 2025. *The Democratic Marketplace: How a More Equal Economy Can Save Our Political Values*. Cambridge, MA: Harvard University Press.

Herzog, L. forthcoming. 'Democratizing Work'. In J. Junker and G. Rozeboom (eds.), *The Oxford Handbook of the Philosophy of Work*.

Herzog, L., and Lepenies, R. 2022. 'Citizen Science in Deliberative Systems: Participation, Epistemic Injustice, and Civic Empowerment'. *Minerva* 60, 489–408.

Herzog, L., and Zacka, B. 2019. 'Fieldwork in Political Theory: Five Arguments for an Ethnographic Sensibility'. *British Journal of Political Science* 49(2), 763–784.

Herzog, L., and Zimmermann, B. 2025. 'Sustainable Work: A Conceptual Map for a Social-Ecological Approach'. *International Labor Review* 164(1), 55–80.

Hickel, Jason. 2020. *Less Is More: How Degrowth Will Save the World*. London: Penguin.

Hirschman, A. O. 1970. *Exit, Voice, and Loyalty: Responses to Decline in Firms, Organizations, and States*. Cambridge, MA: Harvard University Press.

Hochschild, A. 2016. *Strangers in Their own Land: Anger and Mourning on the American Right*. New York: The New Press.

Hoffman, D. A. 2006. 'The Best Puffery Article Ever'. *Iowa Law Review* 91(5), 1395, 101–151.

Honoré, A. M. 1961. 'Ownership'. In A. G. Guest (ed.), *Oxford Essays in Jurisprudence*. Oxford: Oxford University Press, 107–147.

Horkheimer, M. 1937/1968. 'Traditional and Critical Theory'. In *Critical Theory: Selected Essays*. New York: Continuum, 188–252. https://monoskop.org/images/7/74/Horkheimer_Max_Critical_Theory_Selected_Essays_2002.pdf.

Hussain, W. 2020. 'Pitting People against Each Other'. *Philosophy and Public Affairs* 48(1), 79–113.

Iser, M. 'Recognition'. *The Stanford Encyclopedia of Philosophy* (Summer 2019 Edition), Edward N. Zalta (ed.), <https://plato.stanford.edu/archives/sum2019/entries/recognition/>.

Iversen, T., and Soskice, D. 2019. *Democracy and Prosperity: Reinventing Capitalism through a Turbulent Century*. Princeton: Princeton University Press.

Jackson, T. 2021. *Post Growth: Life after Capitalism*. Cambridge: Polity.

Jaeggi, R. 2016. *Alienation*. New York: Columbia University Press.

Kelton, S. 2020. *The Deficit Myth: Modern Monetary Theory and the Birth of the People's Economy*. London: Public Affairs Books.

Khan, L. M. 2017. 'Amazon's Antitrust Paradox'. *The Yale Law Journal* 126(3), 710–805.

Kidd, I. J., and Medina, J. (eds.). 2017. *The Routledge Handbook of Epistemic Injustice*. London: Routledge.

Kim, H. 2019. 'An Extension of Rawls's Theory of Justice for Climate Change'. *International Theory* 11(2), 160–181.

King Jr., Rev. Dr. Martin Luther. 1963/2011. *All Labor Has Dignity*. Boston: Beacon Press.

Kochhar, R. 2023. 'The Enduring Grip of the Gender Pay Gap'. *Pew Research Center*, 1 March, www.pewresearch.org/social-trends/2023/03/01/the-enduring-grip-of-the-gender-pay-gap/.

Kołakowski, L. 2008. *Main Currents of Marxism*. New York: W. W. Norton.

Krouse, R., and McPherson, M. 1986. 'A "Mixed"-Property Regime: Equality and Liberty in a Market Economy'. *Ethics* 97(1), 119–138.

Lafont, C. 2019. *Democracy without Shortcuts: A Participatory Conception of Deliberative Democracy*. New York: Oxford University Press.

Landemore, H., and Ferreras, I. 2016. 'In Defense of Workplace Democracy: Towards a Justification of the Firm–State Analogy'. *Political Theory* 44, 53–81.

Landemore, H. 2020. *Open Democracy: Reinventing Popular Rule for the Twenty-First Century*. Princeton: Princeton University Press.

LeGrand, J. 1990. 'Justice Versus Efficiency: The Elusive Trade-Off'. *Ethics* 3, 554–568.

Lever, A. 2009. 'Is Judicial Review Undemocratic?' *Perspectives on Politics* 7(4), 897–915.

Locke, J. 1689/1988. *Two Treatises of Government*. Ed. Peter Laslett. Cambridge: Cambridge University Press.

Longo, M., and Zacka, B. 2019. 'Political Theory in an Ethnographic Key'. *American Political Science Review* 113(4), 1066–1070.

Lukes, S. 1974/2005. *Power: A Radical View*, 2nd expanded ed. New York: Palgrave.

Lukes, S. 2016. 'Power and Economics'. In R. Skidelsky and N. Craig (eds.), *Who Runs the Economy?* London: Macmillan, 17–25.

Malleson, T. 2023. *Against Inequality: The Practical and Ethical Case for Abolishing the Superrich*. New York: Oxford University Press.

Malmendier, U., and Tate, G. 2009. 'Superstar CEOs'. *The Quarterly Journal of Economics* 124(4), 1593–1638.

Mankiw, N. G. 2010. 'Spreading the Wealth Around: Reflections Inspired by Joe the Plumber'. *Eastern Economic Journal* 36, 285–298.

Manning, A. 2021. 'Monopsony in Labor Markets: A Review'. *ILR Review* 74(1), 3–26.

Martinez-Alier, J. 2002. *Environmentalism of the Poor*. London: Edward Elgar.

Marx, K. 1844/2000. *Economic & Philosophic Manuscripts of 1844*. Marxist.org archive.

Marx, K. 1845/1969. *Thesen über Feuerbach. Marx-Engels Werke Band 3*. Berlin: Dietz Verlag.

Marx. K. 1859/1971. *Zur Kritik der Politischen Ökonomie. Marx-Engels Werke Band 13*. Berlin: Dietz Verlag.

Mas-Colell, A., Whinston, M. D., and Green, J. R. 1995. *Microeconomic Theory*. New York: Oxford University Press.

McAlevey, J. 2016. *No Shortcuts: Organizing for Power in the New Gilded Age*. New York: Oxford University Press.

McMahon, C. 2012. *Public Capitalism: The Political Authority of Corporate Executives*. Philadelphia: University of Pennsylvania Press.

Meiksins Wood, E. 1995. *Democracy against Capitalism: Renewing Historical Materialism*. Cambridge: Cambridge University Press.

Mill, J. S. 2008 [1848/73]. *Principles of Political Economy and Chapters on Socialism*. Oxford: Oxford University Press.

Montesquieu, C.-J. 1989 [1748]. *The Spirit of the Laws*. Trans. A. M. Cohler, B. C. Miller, and H. S. Stone. Cambridge: Cambridge University Press.

More, T. 1967 [1516] . *Utopia*. Trans. J. P. Dolan. In J. J. Greene and J. P. Dolan (eds.), *The Essential Thomas More*. New York: New American Library, pp. 23–96.

Moriarty, J. 2010. 'Participation in the Workplace: Are Employees Special'. *Journal of Business Ethics* 92, 373–384.

Morris, P. 2007. *Power: A Philosophical Analysis*, 2nd ed. Manchester: Manchester University Press.

Mueller, J.-W. 2017. *What Is Populism?* New York: Penguin.

Murphy, L., and Nagel, T. 2002. *The Myth of Ownership: Taxes and Justice*. New York: Oxford University Press.

Narveson, J. 2010. 'Property and Rights'. *Social Philosophy & Policy* 27, 101–134.

Nozick, R. 1974. *Anarchy, State, and Utopia*. New York: Basic Books.

O'Neill, M. 2020a. 'Power, Predistribution, and Social Justice'. *Philosophy* 95(1), 63–91.

O'Neill, M. 2020b. 'Social Justice and Economic Systems'. *Philosophical Topics* 48(2), 159–201.

Oreskes, N., and Eric C. 2010. *Merchants of Doubt: How a Handful of Scientists Obscured the Truth on Issues from Tobacco Smoke to Global Warming*. London: Bloomsbury.

Ostrom, E. 1990. *Governing the Commons: The Evolution of Institutions for Collective Action*. Cambridge: Cambridge University Press.

Parvin, P. 2022. 'Hidden in Plain Sight: How Lobby Organisations Undermine Democracy'. In R. Claassen, M. Bennett, and H. Brouwer (eds.), *Wealth and Power*. London: Routledge, 229–251.

Pateman, C. 1970. *Participation and Democratic Theory*. Cambridge: Cambridge University Press.

Pérotin, V. 2016. 'What Do We Really Know about Worker Co-operatives?' Coop UK. www.uk.coop/sites/default/files/2020-10/worker_co-op_report.pdf.

Pettit, P. 1997. *Republicanism: A Theory of Freedom and Government*. Oxford: Oxford University Press.

Pettit, P. 2006. 'Freedom in the Market'. *Politics, Philosophy & Economics* 5(2), 131–149.

Pfeffer, J. 2018. *Dying for a Paycheck: How Modern Management Harms Employee Health and Company Performance – and What We Can Do about It*. New York: Harper Collins.

Pfeifer, C. 2023. 'Can Worker Codetermination Stabilize Democracies? Works Councils and Satisfaction with Democracy in Germany'. *University of Lüneburg Working Paper Series in Economics*, No. 420.

Philippon, T. 2019. *The Great Reversal: How America Gave up on Free Markets*. Cambridge, MA: Harvard University Press.

Piketty, T. 2014. *Capital in the 21st Century*. Cambridge, MA: Harvard University Press.

Piketty, T. 2020. *Capital and Ideology*. Cambridge, MA: Harvard University Press.

Pistor, K. 2013. 'A Legal Theory of Finance'. *Journal of Comparative Economics* 41(2), 315–330.

Pistor, K. 2019. *The Code of Capital: How the Law Creates Wealth and Inequality*. Princeton: Princeton University Press.

Polanyi, K. 1944. *The Great Transformation*, Boston: Beacon Press.

Pullinger, M., 2014. 'Working Time Reduction Policy in a Sustainable Economy: Criteria and Options for Its Design'. *Ecological Economics* 103, 11–19.

Quiggin, J. 2010. *Zombie Economics: How Dead Ideas Still Walk among Us*. Princeton: Princeton University Press.

Rawls, J. 1971. *A Theory of Justice*. Cambridge, MA: Belknap Press of Harvard University Press.

Rawls, J. 1982. 'Social Unity and Primary Goods'. In A. Sen and B. Williams (eds.), *Utilitarianism and Beyond*. Cambridge: Cambridge University Press, 159–185.

Rawls, J. 1993. *Political Liberalism*. New York: Columbia University Press.

Rawls, J. 1999. *A Theory of Justice*. Revised Edition. Cambridge, MA: The Belknap Press of Harvard University Press.

Rawls, J. 2001. *Justice as Fairness*: *A Restatement*. Cambridge, MA: Harvard University Press.

Reiff, M. R. 2012. 'The Difference Principle, Rising Inequality, and Supply-Side Economics: How Rawls Got Hijacked by the Right'. *Review of Economic Philosophy* 13, 119–173.

Reiff, M. R. 2013. *Exploitation and Economic Justice in the Liberal Capitalist State*. New York: Oxford University Press.

Robeyns, I. 2022. 'Why Limitarianism?' *Journal of Political Philosophy* 30(2), 249–270.

Rockström, J., Steffen, W., Noone, K., et al. 2009. 'A Safe Operating Space for Humanity'. *Nature* 461(7263), 472–475.

Romeo, N. 2022. 'How Mondragon Became the World's Largest Co-OP'. *The New Yorker*, 27 August.

Rossi, E., and Sleat, M. 2014. 'Realism in Normative Political Theory'. *Philosophy Compass* 9(10), 689–701.

Rothstein, B. 2021. When Capitalism Relinquishes Ownership. *Social Europe*, June 25.

Sandberg, J., and Warenski, L. (eds.). 2024. *The Philosophy of Money and Finance*. New York: Oxford University Press.

Sandel, M. J. 2012. *What Money Can't Buy*: *The Moral Limits of Markets*. New York: Farrar Straus Giroux.

Satz, D. 2010. *Why Some Things Should Not Be for Sale*: *The Moral Limits of Markets*. Oxford: Oxford University Press.

Schemmel, C. 2021. *Justice and Egalitarian Relations*. Oxford: Oxford University Press.

Schlachter, L. H., and Ársaelsson, K. M. 2024. 'Civic Work: Making a Difference on and off the Clock'. *American Journal of Sociology* 130(1), 44–87.

Schmidt, A. T. (2017). 'The Power to Nudge'. *American Political Science Review* 111(2), 404–417.

Scholz, R., and Vitols, S. 2019. 'Board-Level Codetermination: A Driving Force for Corporate Social Responsibility in German Companies?' *European Journal of Industrial Relations* 25(3), 233–234.

Schor, J. 1992. *The Overworked American: The Unexpected Decline of Leisure*. New York: Basic Books.

Schor, J. 1998. *The Overspent American*: *Upscaling, Downshifting, and the New Consumer*. New York: Basic Books.

Schwandt, H., and von Wachter, T. 2023. 'Life-Cycle Impacts of Graduating in a Recession'. *NBER Reporter.* Spring.

Schweickart, D. 2011. *After Capitalism.* 2nd ed., Lanham: Rowman & Littlefield.

Sen, A. 1985. 'The Moral Standing of the Market'. *Social Philosophy and Policy* 2(2), 1–19.

Shields, L. 2020. 'Sufficientarianism'. *Philosophy Compass* 15(11), e12704, 1–10.

Shiffrin, S. V. 2014. *Speech Matters: On Lying, Morality, and the Law.* Princeton: Princeton University Press.

Spencer, E. M., Mills, A. E., Rorty, M. V., and Werhane, P. H. 2000. *Organization Ethics in Health Care.* New York: Oxford University Press.

Spiegler, P. 2015. *Behind the Model: A Constructive Critique of Economic Modeling.* Cambridge: Cambridge University Press.

Standing, G. 2011. *The Precariat: The New Dangerous Class.* London: Bloomsbury.

Stansbury, A., and Summers, L. H. 2020. 'The Declining Worker Power Hypothesis: An Explanation for the Recent Evolution of the American Economy'. *NBER Working Paper Series*, No. 27193.

Stevis, D., and Felli, R. 2015. 'Global Labour Unions and Just Transition to a Green Economy'. *International Environmental Agreements* 15, 29–43.

Svampa, M. 2019. *Neo-Extractivism in Latin America: Socio-Environmental Conflicts, the Territorial Turn, and New Political Narratives.* Cambridge: Cambridge University Press.

Tcherneva, P. R. 2020. *The Case for a Job Guarantee.* Cambridge: Polity.

Terzi, A. 2022. *Growth for Good: Reshaping Capitalism to Save Humanity from Climate Catastrophe.* Cambridge, MA: Harvard University Press.

Thomas, A. 2017. *Republic of Equals: Predistribution and Property-Owning Democracy.* New York: Oxford University Press.

Thomas, A., Archer, A., and Engelen, B. 2025. *Extravagance and Misery: The Emotional Regime of Market Societies.* New York: Oxford University Press.

Tobin, J. 1978. 'A Proposal for International Monetary Reform'. *Eastern Economic Journal* 4(3–4), 153–159.

Tomasi, J. 2012. *Free Market Fairness.* Princeton: Princeton University Press.

Töns, J. 2023. *John Rawls and Environmental Justice: Implementing a Sustainable and Socially Just Future.* London: Routledge.

Valentini, L. 2012. 'Ideal vs. Non-Ideal Theory: A Conceptual Map'. *Philosophy Compass* 7(9), 654–664.

Vallentyne, P., Steiner, H., and Otsuka, M. 2005. 'Why Left-Libertarianism Is Not Incoherent, Indeterminate, or Irrelevant: A Reply to Fried'. *Philosophy & Public Affairs* 33(2), 201215.

van Bavel, B. 2016. *The Invisible Hand? How Market Economies Have Emerged and Declined since AD 500*. Oxford: Oxford University Press.

van der Vossen, B., and Christmas, B. 2023. 'Libertarianism'. *The Stanford Encyclopedia of Philosophy*, ed. E. N. Zalta and U. Nodelman (eds.), <https://plato.stanford.edu/archives/fall2023/entries/libertarianism/>.

Vosoughi, S., Roy, D., Aral, S., et al. 2018. 'The Spread of True and False News Online'. *Science* 359(6380), 1146–1151.

Vrousalis, N. 2023. *Exploitation as Domination: What Makes Capitalism Unjust*. New York: Oxford University Press.

Walzer, M. 1983. *Spheres of Justice: A Defense of Pluralism and Equality*. New York: Basic Books.

Weber, M. 1968 [1921]. *Economy and Society: An Outline of Interpretive Sociology*, ed. Guenther Roth. New York: Bedminster Press.

White, S. 2011. 'The Republican Critique of Capitalism'. *Critical Review of International Social and Political Philosophy* 14(5), 561–579.

Williams, A. 1998. 'Incentives, Inequality, and Publicity'. *Philosophy and Public Affairs* 27(3), 225–247.

Williamson, O. E. 1975. *Markets and Hierarchies: Analysis and Antitrust Implications*. New York: The Free Press.

Wright, E. O. 2010. *Envisioning Real Utopias*. London: Verso.

Young, I. M. 2011. *Responsibility for Justice*. New York: Oxford University Press.

Zbyszewska, A., and Maximo, F. 2025. 'Narratives of Sustainable Work in Mining-Affected Communities: Gleaning a Decolonial Concept'. *International Labor Review* 164(1), 1–20.

Cambridge Elements⁼

Political Philosophy

Cécile Laborde
University of Oxford

Cécile Laborde holds the Nuffield Chair in Political Theory at Oxford University. She is the author of *Pluralist Thought and the State* (2000) and *Critical Republicanism* (2008). Her last monograph, *Liberalism's Religion*, was awarded the 2019 Spitz Prize.

Steven Wall
University of Arizona

Steven Wall is a Professor of Philosophy at the University of Arizona. He is a founding editor and currently editor of *Oxford Studies in Political Philosophy*. He is the author of *Liberalism, Perfectionism and Restraint* (Cambridge, 1998) and the editor of *The Cambridge Companion to Liberalism* (Cambridge, 2008).

About the series

Cambridge Elements in Political Philosophy offers concise and original introductions to central topics in political philosophy. A broad understanding of the discipline will include discussions of nations, states and communities, global justice, rights, the practice of politics, power and authority, and politics and social life, and new and emerging issues will be covered as well as more traditional problems. Each Element will provide a balanced survey of the current state of debate on the topic in question as well as presenting a distinctive perspective that advances new ideas and arguments.

Cambridge Elements

Political Philosophy

Elements in the Series

Politics and the Economy
Lisa Herzog

Political Meritocracy in the 21st Century
Brian Kogelmann

Wrongful Discrimination
Kasper Lippert-Rasmussen

A full series listing is available at: www.cambridge.org/EPLP

For EU product safety concerns, contact us at Calle de José Abascal, 56–1°,
28003 Madrid, Spain or eugpsr@cambridge.org.

www.ingramcontent.com/pod-product-compliance
Lightning Source LLC
LaVergne TN
LVHW011855060526
838200LV00054B/4336